Reducing
Finding Peace

Pat Collins CM

VERITAS

Published 2002 by
Veritas Publications
7/8 Lower Abbey Street
Dublin 1
Email publications@veritas.ie
Website www.veritas.ie

A shorter version of the book was first published in 1989 as
Overcoming Stress by All Hallows and Veritas Publications

ISBN 1 85390 621 2

A catalogue record for this book is available from the British Library.

Cover design by Louise Baker
Printed in the Republic of Ireland by Betaprint Ltd, Dublin

*Veritas books are printed on paper made from the wood pulp of managed
forests. For every tree felled, at least one tree is planted, thereby renewing
natural resources.*

Contents

Foreword

I first met Pat Collins about thirty years ago at the Christian Renewal Centre in Rostrevor, where we shared a platform. It was at a time when two major social changes were happening in parallel, both relevant to the subject matter of this book. The first was negative, causing both acute and chronic stress to many people – the early stages of the Northern Ireland 'Troubles'. The second, the Charismatic Renewal Movement, in which Pat was a significant figure, was very positive and liberating for many who had suffered in that other situation. He impressed me as a man with the ability to look at issues in fresh and imaginative ways, combining the intellectual rigour of a scholar and the creativity of the artist with the heart of a pastor. We have found ourselves together in similar situations over the intervening years and I have observed a deepening in his understanding of and empathy with people in troubled states. As will be apparent in this book, it is to no small degree the consequence of his own experience of life with its quota of stresses and strains, at once unique to him and at the same time containing principles of universal relevance. So he writes, not only from a theoretical point of view as one observing the human predicament, but also from 'the coal face' where all of us operate.

Not long ago I attended a men's retreat, along with about two hundred others. The most common answer to an initial question 'What is your main problem at present?' yielded the answer 'stress'. The demand for a new, revised and enlarged edition of this book is testimony both to the continuing and increasing levels of stress in our modern society and to the practical wisdom of its contents.

We are given a helpful description of the various types of stress and the associated physiological responses. Understanding the physical basis of what we experience can, in itself, be comforting. To know that I am not 'going mad' or 'losing my mind' removes one layer of unhelpful stress and helps build a foundation on which a recovery strategy can be built. There follows a description of some of those strategies, some road-tested and attested by the author. They contain much good common sense, backed up by professional opinion and experience.

This text can be read at more than one level. The earlier sections will be helpful to many, regardless of the nature of their religious beliefs, or if they have none. They emphasise strategies aimed at the reduction of the unpleasant and debilitating effects of stress, and touch on lifestyle issues that often underlie the problem. As a medical doctor I am conscious that *dis-ease* is frequently a mere symptom of disease, and that it is inadequate and often dangerous to deal with symptoms while leaving the underlying condition unresolved. The final chapter addresses this issue. The sense of stress may be a warning symptom that we are out of proper relationship with the God who made us, and his purposes for us as creatures in his world. Augustine said 'You have made us for yourself, and we will find no rest till we find our rest in you'. Even more pertinent are the words of Jesus, centuries before, 'Come to me all you who are heavy laden and I will give you rest'. Techniques and strategies may release tension and induce tranquillity, but true peace (Biblical: *shalom*) can only be found in restored relationship with God our Creator and with our fellow creatures. For this we need the reconciling work of Jesus and the inner presence of the Holy Spirit. The final section engages with this, thus emphasising that peace, in the last analysis, is not a primary goal but a side effect of something greater.

I am pleased to be associated with the fresh presentation of this helpful book and believe that it will be of significant help to many in escaping from the vicious cycle of stress-related problems, and in connecting with the ultimate source of our peace – God himself.

Roy Millar BSc, MB, FRCS (Ed)
(Formerly Consultant Surgeon, Royal Victoria Hospital, Belfast)

Introduction

I wrote a booklet entitled *Overcoming Stress* at the end of the eighties. Even then there was a real need for resources that would help Irish people to reduce the strain they were experiencing. The country was going through a hard time economically. Unemployment was high, at one stage it reached about eighteen per cent. Tens of thousands of our people, especially young men and women, had to leave the country in search of work. Remember how the limited number of green cards, which were necessary for entry into the United States, were so eagerly sought after. I can recall a discussion about the national debt on the *Late Late Show*. If my memory serves me correctly it was over £20 billion (€25.4 billion) at the time. The interest being paid, *per annum*, was said to be equivalent to all the VAT collected in a twelve month period. Some of Gay Byrne's guests were predicting that the Republic was headed for bankruptcy. Even more jobs would be lost. Our standard of living would decline. The numbers leaving the country would increase.

Since then, the Celtic Tiger unexpectedly came into our lives. The economy turned around. Taxes and unemployment fell and wages went up. Economists say that we will continue to enjoy growth. As a result we can expect to become one of the wealthier countries in the EU. Whereas, recession was the main cause of stress in the 80s, in the early twenty-first century accelerating growth is the problem.

As commentators have noted, we have a first world economy and a third world infrastructure. We haven't the houses, roads, railways and transport systems to cope with the demands of an increasing population and an expanding economy. House prices and rents have shot up, traffic jams have increased, the pace and pressure of everyday life have become more hectic. Besides these changes, increasing numbers of people have drifted away from institutional forms of Christianity. Traditional beliefs and values are increasingly called into question. Instead of living within the context of the shared meanings that once gave cohesion to society, our postmodern, pluralist culture is more fragmented and disillusioned. Consequently, people tend to be more insecure. Although all of the changes have undoubtedly had an up side, there is an obvious down-side as well. There are more uncertainties and pressures than ever. Many Irish people suffer from unhealthy levels of stress. Professor Anthony Clare has succinctly described the situation as 'what we experience when there is a significant lack of balance between the resources we possess and the demands made on us'. One of the disturbing signs of this lack of balance is the rising suicide rate, especially among young men.

In the autumn of 2001, research conducted on behalf of the Mental Health Association of Ireland revealed that around thirty-five per cent of the respondents had experienced elevated levels of stress in the recent past. Seventy-three per cent of those who answered the questionnaire said that life in Ireland was more stressful than it had been five years before. The main causes of this stress were financial worries, health problems, transport difficulties and pressures at work. People in the 35-44 year old group were the ones most likely to say that life was more stressful. Apparently, Dublin is not only the national capital, but the capital of stress as well. It is closely followed by the province of Leinster, while people in Munster report the least amount of stress. These figures confirm the common sense observation that, despite many improvements, life in Ireland is more stressful than in the past.

Overcoming Stress has been renamed. This expended edition is called *Reducing Stress and Finding Peace* because I don't think that it is either desirable, or possible, to get rid of all stress. A certain level of healthy stress is necessary if we wish to realise our full potential, for example, in sporting activities. In this short book I hope not only to provide readers with an understanding of the nature and causes of chronic stress, but also to suggest a number of practical ways of reducing it. The approach is psycho-spiritual in so far as it tries to integrate psychological insights with Christian beliefs. It does so in the firm belief that the grace of God builds upon and completes our natural potential. As Edward Charlesworth and Ronald Nathan, the authors of a secular book entitled *Stress Management*, observe: 'Religious fellowship, spiritual principles, and faith in something greater than man can be major sources of strength for daily living and times of crisis.' In recent times there has been a rapid growth in books and articles that explore the connection between medicine and spirituality. I have provided a brief survey entitled 'Is Prayer Good for Your Health?' in *The Broken Image: Reflections on Spirituality and Culture* (Dublin: Columba, 2002), pp. 86-92. This book is dedicated to the memory of my uncles, Drs Paddy and Jack Kelly.

The Nature of Stress

A few years ago I headed off with two colleagues to conduct a parish mission. Normally I would have been enthusiastic. But not on this occasion. Instead I dreaded the prospect of meeting strangers and dealing with their many problems. On our very first morning in the parish I got off to a bad start. I became quite abrasive with a woman who had annoyed me. Afterwards I felt rotten. Why had I lost my self-control in such an unreasonable and insensitive way? I began to realise that I did not feel well. I was tense, up-tight and reluctant to face any kind of pressure. So I came to a difficult and embarrassing decision. It would be better for the team, the parishioners and myself if I withdrew from the mission. For the next few months I felt miserable. I could not sleep well. I always felt tired. I got many dull headaches. They could last for days and were unaffected by aspirin. I felt anxious and apprehensive all the time. On one or two occasions I felt a real sense of panic. Over and over again, I asked myself the question, 'What is happening to me?' I did not really know, but I was determined to find out.

Then as a result of a lot of reading and reflection, I came to recognise that I was suffering from 'burnout'. It is a form of emotional exhaustion that is brought on by unhealthy levels of unrelieved stress. Some of it had been triggered by outer environmental factors such as the demanding nature of my work. Still more had been occasioned by inward psychological causes such as an exaggerated fear of failure.

But there was reason for hope. I began to realise that the pain of stress is nature's red light. It was warning me that the way I was living was not working. It was inviting me to make the necessary psychological and environmental changes that would help me to recover. Over a period of time I came to terms with these issues. I learned to relax and so regained my sense of personal well being and peace.

Carl Jung once wrote: 'There is no growth in consciousness without pain.' Looking back, I can see how the experience of stress was for me a blessing in disguise. It forced me to take stock in many ways. As a result I grew in self-awareness and made a number of practical changes in my lifestyle. St Paul says that we are comforted in our troubles 'so that we may be able to comfort those who are in any trouble with the comfort with which we ourselves are comforted' (2 Cor 1:4). Hence these pages are written in the belief that, if you or someone you care about suffers from unhealthy levels of stress, it can and should be reduced. Stress is an invitation to change and to grow.

WHAT IS STRESS?

Put simply, stress is nervous tension. Professor Lightman, an expert on the subject, says that: 'Stress occurs when a human being experiences any threat to his or her physical integrity or mental well-being.' A more comprehensive definition would describe stress as the discomfort felt by a person or group when under pressure, which may show itself in physiological, emotional and behavioural ways. It can also refer to the source of the pressure itself, what is referred to as the *stressor*. We have already noted that stress can be caused by environmental and psychological factors. These can lead to either *acute* or *chronic* stress. Stress is acute when it is sharp but short-lived. By and large, it doesn't do us much harm. Indeed it may be helpful in the sense that it adds an extra edge to our performance, e.g. when doing an exam or acting in a play. Stress becomes chronic when it persists in an unrelieved way. Combining these points we can look at a number of examples

1. *Acute environmental stress* could be experienced when a person has to move quickly to catch a valuable vase as it falls from the mantelpiece.

2. *Chronic environmental stress* could be experienced by a person who has to work in an extremely noisy factory.

3. *Acute psychological stress* could occur as a result of hiccupping during an important speech.

4. *Chronic psychological stress* could be the outcome of having to cope with a bad marriage to an alcoholic partner.

So stress can be triggered by any number of factors. Clearly, there are more of them than ever in contemporary society where the demands of everyday life seems to increase all the time. In the cities we have to cope with such things as incessant phone calls, long queues, information overload, and so on. Commenting on the world of work, Professor Cary Cooper, an expert on stress, says: 'In the past decade there has been a constant Americanisation of the British and Irish workforces. This has meant more job insecurity, longer hours, workaholism, lack of work/life balance and an autocratic management style. Workers traditionally accepted job insecurity in exchange for a nine-to-five working day, but now that contract has been broken.' Cooper points out that nowadays a lot of work is sub contracted. People are employed to do a particular task, but they do not have long term job security. All of this uncertainty tends to increase people's feelings of stress. Joe Armstrong has pointed out, in a booklet entitled *Workplace Stress in Ireland,* that such distress arises when the demands of the job exceed people's capacity to meet them. Job stress is often confused with challenge, but these concepts are not the same. Challenge energises us psychologically and physically, and it motivates us to learn new skills and master our jobs. Unhealthy stress does neither. Work related stress can be aggravated by things such as badly organised shifts and structures, changes in the workplace, poor relationships and communication, lack of personal control over the task, ill-defined roles, dull, repetitive assignments, highly demanding tasks, dealing directly with the public and the threat of harassment or even violence.

In the last analysis, however, stress is a largely subjective event – it *depends on the person's reaction more than on outside events.* That said, the experience of stress is always the same. Nature has equipped us to cope with perceived dangers. In an emergency situation the body goes on red alert. Automatically the brain triggers a sequence of physiological changes. Hormones are produced. Digestion slows. Blood pressure rises. Perspiration increases. The eyeballs retract, while the pupils, nostrils and bronchi dilate. Sugars and fats are secreted to provide the body with extra energy. Muscles grow tense, ready for 'flight or fight'. This primitive reaction was very helpful when our ancestors had to cope with life and death situations. After all, they had to face regular attacks from either animals, enemies or unpredictable natural events such as earthquakes, floods and volcanoes. It gave them the extra strength they needed to take appropriate action such as fighting or running away. As a result of their vigorous efforts their emergency supplies of energy were used up, and so they returned to a state of relaxation.

While the challenges and demands of modern life are many, they are rarely life-threatening. Even when they are, e.g. having to brake suddenly in order to avoid an accident, we do not really need the extra surge of energy the body supplies. All we have to do is to move one foot to jam on the brakes. When the emergency has passed we remain up-tight because we have not used up our extra quotient of energy. The same is true when we are faced by the lesser crises of everyday life, such as meeting deadlines, keeping appointments, paying bills, etc. As a result our 'flight or fight' response is activated over and over again in an unnecessary way. Stress levels go up and acute stress becomes chronic.

Symptoms of Stress

Physical symptoms involving skeletal muscles
1. Tension headaches
2. Frowning
3. Grinding teeth
4. Jaw pain
5. Stuttering or stammering
6. Trembling of lips or hands
7. Muscle tenseness and aches
8. Neck aches
9. Back pain
10. Aggressive body language

Physical symptoms of stress influencing the autonomic nervous system
1. Migraine headaches
2. Increased sensitivity to light and sound
3. Light-headedness, dizziness
4. Ringing in the ears
5. Enlarged pupils
6. Blushing
7. Dry mouth
8. Problems swallowing
9. Frequent colds and bouts of flu
10. Hives
11. Rashes
12. Heartburn, stomach cramps or nausea.
13. Uneven or rapid heartbeat without exercising
14. Difficulty breathing
15. Sudden feelings of panic, as if one was about to die
16. Heat and chest pain
17. Increased perspiration
18. Night sweats
19. Cold, sweaty hands
20. Painfully cold hands and feet

21. Flatulence and belching
22. Frequent urination
23. Constipation
24. Nervous diarrhoea
25. Lowered sexual desire
26. Difficulty in reaching sexual climax

Mental symptoms of stress
1. Anxiety, worry, guilt or nervousness
2. Increased propensity to anger and frustration
3. Moodiness
4. Depression
5. Increased or decreased appetite
6. Racing thoughts
7. Nightmares
8. Problems concentrating
9. Difficulties learning new information
10. Forgetfulness
11. Disorganisation
12. Difficulty making decisions
13. A sense of being overloaded or overwhelmed by problems
14. A tendency to cry more often than normal
15. Suicidal thoughts
16. Fear of getting close to people
17. Loneliness

Behavioural symptoms of stress
1. Inattention to ones dress or grooming
2. Frequent un-punctuality
3. A more serious frowning appearance
4. Unusual behaviour
5. Nervous habits such as finger and foot tapping
6. Rushing around or pacing the floor in a nervous way
7. Edginess
8. Over reaction to small things

9. Increased number of small accidents
10. Perfectionism
11. Reduced work efficiency or productivity
12. Lies and excuses to cover up inefficiency
13. Fast or mumbled speech
14. Defensiveness or suspiciousness
15. Strained communication with others
16. Social withdrawal
17. Constant tiredness
18. Sleep problems
19. Frequent use of over-the-counter drugs
20. Weight gain or loss without diet
21. Increased smoking
22. Recreational drug use
23. Increased alcohol use
24. Gambling or overspending

A SIMPLE STRESS TEST

At the Gershom Centre in England, clients are given the following list of twenty signs of stress and asked to tick off the ones they are currently experiencing. Why not do the test yourself?

1.	Rheumatic pains	11.	Dizziness
2.	Swollen glands	12.	Palpitations
3.	Breathlessness	13.	Blackouts
4.	Tingling sensations	14.	Insomnia
5.	Diarrhoea	15.	Headaches or migraine
6.	Urinary & gynaecological problems	16.	Exhaustion problems
7.	Stomach pains	17.	Allergies
8.	Asthma	18.	Nausea
9.	Mouth Ulcers	19.	Tension
10.	Depression	20.	Skin rashes

If you are suffering from four or more of these symptoms for a period of a month or more you may be suffering from unhealthy levels of stress. If it remains unrelieved it can have harmful physical, psychological and spiritual effects.

STRESSFUL LIFE EVENTS SURVEY

In 1967 F. H. Holmes and R. H. Rahe published the frequently quoted 'The Social Readjustment Rating Scale' in the *Journal of Psychometric Research*. It listed stressful life events and accorded each one a number of specified points. Have a look at the list and tick off the ones that ring a bell for you. When you get to the end add up the number of points you have accumulated. Don't take the points too seriously. They are averages. As you will see, it is clear that a person who hears that s/he has a deadly form of cancer and has only two weeks to live would probably experience more stress than a grandson or granddaughter who hears that his or her 96 year old granddad has died in Australia.

Life Event	Points
Death of a spouse	100
Divorce	73
Birth of a handicapped child	65
Marital separation	65
Jail term	63
Death of a close family member	63
Personal injury or illness	53
Marriage	50
Sacked from work	47
Marital reconciliation	45
Retirement	45
Change in family member's health	44
Pregnancy	40
Sex difficulties	39
Addition to the family	39
Business readjustment	39

Change in financial status	38
Death of a close friend	37
Change to a different kind of work	36
Change in the number of marital arguments	35
Mortgage or loan over 180,000	31
Foreclosure of mortgage or loan	30
Change in work responsibilities	29
Son or daughter leaving home	29
Trouble with in-laws	29
Outstanding personal achievement	28
Spouse begins or stops working	26
Starting or finishing school	26 -
Change in living conditions	25
Revision of personal habits e.g. giving up smoking	24
Trouble with the boss	23
Change in work hours or conditions	20
Change of residence	20
Change in schools	20
Change in recreational habits	19
Change in Church activities	19
Change in social activities	18
Change in sleeping habits	16
Change in number of family gatherings	15
Change in eating habits	15
Holidays	13
Christmas season	12
Minor violations of the law	11
Total	

Add your points. A high reading would be 300 or more. A low number would be 150 or less. Research has indicated that those who experience a high rate of stress are more likely to get ill.

Some Causes and Effects of Stress

TRANSITIONAL CRISES AND STRESS

While we can experience stress at any time in our lives, it is more likely to occur during times of painful change. Cardinal Newman once observed that 'to live is to change'. This is biologically true. Apparently every cell within us is replaced every seven years or so. We change psychologically and spiritually also. This is particularly true during times of personal crisis. These are *the* turning points for better or for worse in our lives.

There are two main types of crisis, *predictable* and *unpredictable*. Psychologists say that *predictable crises* occur regularly throughout our lives. They precede the main developmental phases, e.g. before the onset of early, middle and late adulthood. Daniel Levinson says that these transitions can occur in and around the ages of 17 to 22, 40 to 45, and 60 and 65 approximately. He also indicates that we can expect lesser transitions between the ages of 28 and 33, and again between 50 and 55 approximately. The purpose of these crises is to urge us to tackle some specific developmental task. By doing so we grow into a new depth of maturity. *Unpredictable crises* occur when 'the slings and arrows of outrageous fortune' come our way. We may be pitched into a period of turmoil and soul-searching by the death of a close relative, the news that we have cancer or the loss of our job. Often a predictable crisis will occur at the same time as one or two unpredictable ones. Transitional crises of either kind have a threefold structure.

1. Onset of restlessness
A woman could face a predictable crisis with the onset of the menopause. At the same time she might have to cope with the fact that her husband has lost his job and that her unmarried daughter has become pregnant. Like countless other people she enters a time of painful transition. She may feel that she is losing control over her life. She lives in a sort of emotional 'no man's land' where things happen to her. She feels like a victim. Troubling feelings seep up from the unconscious levels of her experience, e.g. anxiety, fear, insecurity, guilt, confusion, mild depression, etc. She enters a stressful period because her life seems subject to anonymous threats that evoke her 'flight or fight' response on a daily if not an hourly basis.

2. Darkness and exploration
Times of crisis for a woman like this are often times of disillusionment. The way she looked at herself and her priorities is challenged. Beliefs and values that sustained her in the past seem strangely inadequate now. Not surprisingly, she loses her inner sense of joy and peace. Instead she feels agitated and restless. As the scaffolding that supported her self-image is removed, there can be a real sense of loss and grief. Her consciousness of hurt may give rise to a feeling of anger with herself, with others, and perhaps with God. Like many others she may try to repress these feelings. As a result they could turn inwards and attack her, thereby making her feel more insecure, inadequate and helpless. This kind of dynamic can lead to a lot of strain and tension.

During a crisis all kinds of questions surface:

* Why is my self-esteem so low?
* Why is it that I am always trying to please others and to win their approval?
* Why am I a perfectionist and so hard on myself when I fail?
* Why am I driven by a sense of obligation, rather than being motivated by personal conviction?
* Why am always in a hurry with too many things to do?
* Why do I have so little time for friends or leisure activities?

- How come I cannot stand up for myself and assert my dignity and rights when I am being badly treated?
- When there is an argument or conflict of any kind, why do I need peace at any price?

Many other questions like these can arise during a time of transition. They are important. They may be pointing to the largely unconscious attitudes and assumptions that have been causing so much stress in our lives.

3. Resolution and restabilisation

As our defence mechanisms begin to crumble during a time of crisis, we may get in touch with basic questions to do with our identity and values. As we answer them we begin to let go of our former assumptions and attitudes. As we do so, we embrace more appropriate and realistic ones. For example, the menopausal woman with family problems may discover that all her life she has been too preoccupied with public opinion. As she becomes more inner-directed, her sense of security increases while her feelings of stress grow weaker.

FEELINGS OF FRUSTRATION

Stress can be the result of the frustration we feel when we are prevented, for one reason or another, from doing what we want to do. We can react by becoming angry, impatient, and combative. Daniel and George Everly have devised a useful stressful frustration test. It first appeared in *Controlling Stress and Tension: A Holistic Approach* (1979).

Scoring
Nos 1 and 10: a = 1, b = 2, c = 3, d = 4.
Nos 2 to 9: a = 4, b= 3, c = 2, d = 1.

1. When I can't do something the way I'd like to do it, I simply adjust and do it the easiest way.
A. Almost always true
B. Often true
C. Seldom true
D. Almost never true

2. I get upset when someone in front of me drives slowly.
A. Almost always true
B. Often true
C. Seldom true
D. Almost never true

3. It bothers me when my plans are dependant on the action or inaction of others.
A. Almost always true
B. Often true
C. Seldom true
D. Almost never true

4. Whenever possible, I tend to avoid large crowds.
A. Almost always true
B. Often true
C. Seldom true
D. Almost never true

5. I am uncomfortable when I have to stand in long queues.
A. Almost always true
B. Often true
C. Seldom true
D. Almost never true

6. Arguments and conflict situations upset me.
A. Almost always true
B. Often true

C. Seldom true

D. Almost never true

7. When my plans don't work out as smoothly as I expected I become anxious.
A. Almost always true
B. Often true
C. Seldom true
D. Almost never true

8. I require a lot of space to live and work in.
A. Almost always true
B. Often true
C. Seldom true
D. Almost never true

9. When I am busy at some task I hate to be disturbed.
A. Almost always true
B. Often true
C. Seldom true
D. Almost never true

10. I believe that 'all good things are worth waiting for'.
A. Almost always true
B. Often true
C. Seldom true
D. Almost always never true

A-TYPE BEHAVIOUR

In recent years a good deal of research has been done on what is referred to as the A-type personality. It is particularly prone to stress. Two of the most famous investigators in this area were Drs Friedman and Rosenman. They did their ground-breaking work in the early

1960s. They described A-type behaviour as: 'an action-emotion complex that can be observed in any person who is aggressively involved in a chronic, incessant struggle to achieve more and more in less and less time, and if required to do so, against the opposing efforts of other things or persons.' It goes without saying that modern market economies tend to encourage and reward this kind of A-type behaviour.

A-type individuals tend to move, walk, eat, and talk rapidly. They are inclined to emphasise their words and hurry to complete their sentences. They are impatient with the rate at which things happen, interrupt others when they are talking, and find it hard to wait for people to complete tasks they could finish more quickly and more effectively themselves. A-types try to do a number of things at a time, such as answering the phone while writing an unrelated note on paper, or they may read the newspaper while eating breakfast. A-types are very competitive and high achievers. They are driven by a desire to outdo others in getting qualifications, promotion, possessions, and friends. The implicit motto of A-types is 'we try harder.' The opposite to the A-type we have been describing is the B-type personality. It is more laid back and relaxed. It is not time conscious, nor driven. It can look at things more adaptively and think through how to deal with situations. This kind of person is much less vulnerable to unhealthy levels of stress.

If you want to assess whether you are an A- or B- Type personality, answer the following questions devised by Charlesworth and Nathan and published in *Stress Management* (1984). Give yourself a score between 1 and 10 for each question. On a spectrum of 1-10 where do you think you stand? 1-5 would favour the questions on the left hand, whereas 6-10 would favour the questions on the right hand.

Questions	Points
Do you work regular hours? *or* Do you work late or bring work home with you?	
Are you inclined to wait patiently? *or* Do you wait impatiently?	
Are you non competitive? *or* Are you very competitive?	

Do you express your feelings with ease? *or* Are you inclined to bottle up your feelings?

Do you feel limited responsibility? *or* Do you always feel responsible?

Do you rarely get angry? *or* Do you get angry easily and often?

Are you unhurried? *or* Are you always in a hurry?

Is it unusual for you to set deadlines? *or* Do you often set deadlines?

Are you too concerned with precise details? *or* Are you careful about detail?

Have you many interests? *or* Is work your main interest?

Do you try to satisfy inner standards? *or* Do you want the approval of others?

Do you speak in a slow relaxed way? *or* Do you speak in a hurried way?

Can you leave things unfinished for a time? *or* Must you always finish tasks?

Are you satisfied with your job? *or* Are you always striving for something better?

Are you a good listener? *or* Are you inclined to finish sentences for others?

Are you easygoing? *or* Are you a compulsive and driven person?

Do you do things slowly? *or* Are you inclined to do everything quickly?

Do you do one thing at a time? *or* Are you inclined to be thinking of what comes next?

Total

160-200 would be a very high A-type score

135-139, would warrant a high A-yype score

100-134 would deserve a mixture of A- and B-yype

100 or less would be a B-type score.

PANIC ATTACKS

Extreme stress can lead to hyperventilation and the onset of what are known as *panic attacks*. They are a form of acute anxiety. They strike at least 1.6 per cent of the population, and are twice as common in women as in men. They can appear at any age, in children or in the elderly. But, more often than not, they begin in young adults. Interestingly, the English word is derived from *pan*, the Greek God, who suddenly appeared to unsuspecting travellers in the woods, causing them to 'panic'. A woman who suffered from this acute form of stress described the experience as follows:

> For me, a panic attack is almost a violent experience. I feel like I'm going insane. It makes me feel like I'm losing control in a very extreme way. My heart pounds really hard, things seem unreal, and there's this very strong feeling of impending doom.... In between attacks there is this dread and anxiety that it's going to happen again. It can be very debilitating, trying to escape those feelings of panic.
> *(Taken from The Anxiety Panic Internet Resource*
> *www.algy.com/anxiety/panic.html)*

Panic attacks are characterised by the sudden onset of intense anxiety accompanied by physical signs, such as difficulty in breathing, sweating, palpitations, and so on. The attack may recur either infrequently or several times a week. People who suffer from panic attacks can't predict when another will occur. Many of them develop intense insecurity between episodes, worrying when and where the next one will strike. While most attacks average a couple of minutes, occasionally they can go on for up to 10 minutes. In rare cases, they may even last an hour or more.

Panic attack symptoms
- Pounding heart
- Chest pains
- Light-headedness or dizziness
- Nausea or stomach problems
- Flushes or chills
- Shortness of breath or a feeling of smothering or choking
- Tingling or numbness
- Shaking or trembling

- Feelings of unreality
- Terror
- A feeling of being out of control or going crazy
- Fear of dying
- Sweating

Some people who suffer from panic attacks go on to develop panic-attack disorder. This condition is often accompanied by other problems such as depression or alcoholism, and may spawn phobias, which can develop in places or situations where panic attacks have previously occurred. For example, if an attack strikes while a person is going up or down in a lift, s/he may develop a fear of lifts and perhaps start avoiding them. As a result, some people's lives become greatly restricted. They avoid normal, everyday activities such as shopping, driving, or in some cases even leaving the house. When people's routines become so restricted by the disorder, as happens for about one-third of those with panic disorder, the condition is called agoraphobia which literally means 'fear of the market place'. A tendency toward panic attack disorder runs in families. Nevertheless, early treatment can often stop such attacks developing into agoraphobia. Those who suffer in this way should seek professional treatment. Otherwise, the disorder can become very disabling. Studies have shown that a combination of psychotherapy and medications can help 80 to 90 per cent of those afflicted in this way. Significant improvement is usually seen within 6 to 8 weeks. Among the medications that can be helpful are

- *antidepressants* such as fluoxetine, sertraline, paroxetine, fluvoxamine, and citalopram;

- *benzodiazepines* such as diazepam, lorazepam, clonazepam, and alprazolam. For more information on this subject visit www.paems.com.au on the internet.

POST-TRAUMATIC STRESS DISORDER

Those who watch old black and white movies will be familiar with the notion of 'shell shock'. It was a kind of nervous condition that was experienced by soldiers who were exposed to the horrors of battle, e.g. the men who fought in the trenches during Word War 1. This anxiety state is characterised by

1. Hypersensitivity to stimuli such as noises, movements and light. It is accompanied by responses such as involuntary defensive jerking or jumpy movements.

2. Easy irritability progressing even to acts of violence.

3. Sleep disturbances including an inability to get to sleep. When the person does so, it is upset by dreams of battle and nightmares. Post-traumatic stress disorder (PTSD) is quite similar to shell shock. It can be defined as the development of characteristic symptoms after experiencing a psychologically traumatic event that is beyond the range of normal human experience.

In this condition symptoms develop within an individual after s/he has experienced a psychologically overpowering and threatening experience. The traumatic event can include serious automobile accidents, rape, assault, being taken as a hostage, or being caught up in natural disasters such as floods, fires, famines and earthquakes. This extremely stressful disorder can kick in after a number of days, or even months later. There may be a predisposition to develop the illness because of one's prior history, genetic weaknesses, personality traits, or pre-existing emotional problems. A feature of this disorder is the person's propensity to re-experience the traumatic event in nightmares and in intrusive daytime fantasies. Sometimes an insignificant event, like a knock at the door, will trigger off a sudden horrifying recollection of the traumatic event with associated feelings of terror and panic. Other symptoms include emotional numbing, anxiety and depression. There is often a diminished ability to enjoy activities or relationships that were previously pleasurable. Not surprisingly, those afflicted in this way often find it difficult to get a good night's sleep. Among the long-term symptoms of post-traumatic stress disorder are marital and family problems, difficulties at work, and the abuse of alcohol and other drugs. The emotional symptoms usually lessen within six months of onset. However, in some cases they may persist for a long time after the traumatic event that triggered them. Early treatment by a skilled psychotherapist can be very helpful in curing this form of anxiety disorder. The medications that help to lessen panic attacks can also be helpful in lessening PTSD. If you want more information on this rather specialist subject there is an excellent site on the internet at: www.mentalhealth.com/dis/p20-an06.html

PHOBIAS

Many people suffer from free floating anxiety. In other words they are afraid of everything in general and nothing in particular. People who are phobic seem to focus their generalised anxiety on to specific objects or situations for relatively short periods of time. Their phobias involve irrational or excessive fears. In the *Readers Digest Reverse Dictionary* there is a list of 73 different phobias. They vary from more common ones such as *agoraphobia,* the fear of open spaces mentioned in the section on panic attacks; *claustrophobia,* a fear of confined spaces; *arachnaphobia,* a fear of spiders; *astrapophobia,* a fear of lightening; *xenophobia,* a fear of foreigners; *ailurophobia,* a fear of cats; *maniaphobia,* a fear of madness; to less common phobias such as *taphophobia,* a fear of being buried alive; *dromophobia,* a fear of streets or crossing streets; and *triskaidekaphobia,* a fear of the number thirteen. A researcher called Isaac Marks found in 1970 that 5 per cent of the out-patients attending Maudsley Hospital in London were suffering from phobias. Here are some of their common symptoms.

- Feelings of panic, dread, horror, or terror
- Recognition that the fear goes beyond normal boundaries and the actual threat of danger
- Reactions that are automatic and uncontrollable, practically taking over the person's thoughts
- Rapid heartbeat, shortness of breath, trembling, and an overwhelming desire to flee the situation – all the physical reactions associated with extreme fear
- Extreme measures taken to avoid the feared object or situation

I have found that people who suffer from phobias experience stress in two interrelated ways. Firstly, there is the tension that is caused by the anticipatory fear of the thing or situation that evokes their high anxiety such as a social phobia where the person fears that s/he will be embarrassed or humiliated in a public place, speaking at a meeting, or having a drink with colleagues. Incidentally this kind of phobia often afflicts younger, shyer people. Secondly, there is the even higher tension that is evoked when the person is in the situation s/he fears most. The person can experience acute stress, so much so that s/he perspires heavily, goes white as a sheet, experiences a greatly increased heart rate, and is unable to pay attention to conversations and the like.

Experts have tried to alleviate phobias by using different methods, such as implosive therapy and flooding, systematic desensitisation, and aversion therapy together with psychotherapy, and Frankl's paradoxical intention. I have briefly described some of them in chapter six of *Finding Faith in Troubled Times* (1993). Suffice it to say that the people who seem to get the best results are those who use behaviour modification rather than psychotherapy. In behaviour therapy, one meets with a trained therapist who helps the phobic person to confront the feared object or situation in a carefully planned, gradual way, in order to progressively learn to control the physical reaction of fear. The person first imagines the feared object or situation, e.g. flying, works up to looking at pictures that depict the object or situation, and finally actually experiences the situation or comes in contact with the feared object. By confronting rather than fleeing from the object of fear, the person becomes accustomed to it and can lose the terror, horror, panic, and dread he or she once felt.

Medications are also used to control the panic experienced during a phobic situation as well as the anxiety aroused by anticipation of that situation. They are the treatment of first choice for social phobia. According to the American Psychiatric Association any phobia that interferes with daily living and creates extreme disability should be treated. With proper care, the vast majority of phobia patients can overcome their fears and be symptom free for years, if not for life. For more information see the internet site, www.psych.org

Some Psychosomatic Effects of Chronic Stress

Let us start with a brief look at the stress response from a medical point of view. The hypothalamus is the section of the brain that organises the stress response. It sends messages down through the spinal cord, which then connect to the middle of the adrenal medulla, and it releases a hormone called adrenaline. Adrenaline is an important hormone in the stress response. It increases the amount of sugar in the blood. It is a very important protective hormone in the stress situation. The hypothalamus also sends other messages to the pituitary gland, and from the pituitary to the adrenal gland, and this makes cortisol. It is very useful in the short term. Among other things, it turns stored carbohydrates into sugar, which enables people to run faster. But in the long term cortisol secretion is a bad thing. It makes bones weaker and more prone to fracture. It causes neurons in the brain to show signs of degeneration. It causes other changes in the immune system, which probably result in the person being more liable to catch various infectious diseases. So it is a great hormone in the short term, but in the long term it is bad news because of its negative effects.

Stress can directly cause or aggravate such problems as high blood-pressure, which afflicts nearly one in every five of the population. This in turn can lead to kidney disease, strokes and heart failure. There is clear evidence that A-type behaviour, described already, makes heart disease more likely because the stress involved leads to a build-up of cholesterol and a higher likelihood of blood clots. Needless to say, all of these conditions can be life-threatening. Stress can also cause gastrointestinal problems such as peptic ulcers, which are caused by excess amounts of gastric juice, or unusual sensitivity in the lining of the stomach that causes nausea and pain. Other stress related stomach problems include inflammatory disease of the colon and bowel, such as ulcerative colitis and enteritis. Some doctors think that stress can, in some cases, lead to anorexia nervosa, which is a refusal to eat enough food. It is most commonly experienced by adolescent girls.

Chronic stress can aggravate conditions such as backache, arthritis, asthma, multiple sclerosis, allergies, pimples, hyperthyroidism and skin conditions such as rashes. It weakens the body's defence system. As a result it can leave people more vulnerable to infections of all kinds, e.g. from the common cold and flu through to cancer. It is estimated by the medical profession that up to 80 per cent of all sickness is stress-related.

The Signs of Psychological Stress

There are many signs of psychological tension, such as low self-esteem, sleeping difficulties, feeling anxious, social fears, and fears of heights, darkness and being alone.

The effects of chronic psychological stress
People may suffer from the panic attacks already mentioned. They find it hard to *cope* with any pressure and suffer from outbursts of impatience, anger and hostility. Their concentration slips, they make mistakes more often, e.g. locking the keys in the car while the engine is running! Mental blocks are common, e.g. forgetting appointments and names. Sleep is disturbed by many dreams and nightmares. Afterwards sufferers get up feeling tired and tense. Victims of stress may try to escape the pain of their condition in ways that reinforce the problem. Eating has been called 'nature's tranquilliser', what some wit referred to as 'stew and chew'. If stressed people eat too much they will feel guilty as their weight goes up. As a result their self-esteem will drop while their stress levels will rise.

Many people suffering from stress feel thirsty, so they drink endless cups of coffee and tea. Both tannin and caffeine are stimulants that increase stress. Many people try to deaden the pain of stress with alcohol. It is true that it may relax a person for a time. It can make it easier to get off to sleep, but the sleep will be shallow as a result, and so the drinker will get up feeling tired and ill-equipped to meet the challenges of a new day. In some cases alcohol abuse can lead to addiction, accidents, domestic strife, and loss of job, all of which are stressful. In an emergency situation tranquillisers and sleeping pills can be helpful, if they are prescribed for a short period, i.e. six weeks at the most. But if the stressful person comes to rely on them they become part of the problem instead of being part of the solution. It is commonly thought that smoking has a tranquillising effect. Perhaps the oral activity, reminiscent of being breast fed, is reassuring, but nicotine is a stimulant and so increases stress. Many of the illnesses that come from smoking, such as lung cancer and emphysema, don't do much for stress levels either. Chronic stress can lead to all kinds of physical problems, e.g. irregular periods in women and impotence in men. These difficulties reinforce stressful feelings.

STRESS AND BURNOUT

Unrelieved stress can lead to 'burnout'. This term was first coined by Herbert J. Freudenberger in an article in the *Journal of Social Issues* (Vol. 30, 1974). It described staff burnout in helping institutions. Freudenberger defined it as a state of fatigue or frustration brought about by a devotion to a cause, a way of life, or a relationship that failed to produce the expected reward. It is a problem born of good intentions, because it happens when people try to reach unattainable goals and end up depleting their energy and losing touch with themselves and others. The onset is slow and usually unnoticed. It is sometimes referred to as 'compassion fatigue' or emotional exhaustion, because it is most commonly experienced by those who are engaged in helping professions where there is a good deal of emotional involvement with others.

A technical definition of this condition says that burnout is an exhausted, even chronic, emotional response of people involved in stressful, person-to-person helping or service professions. It results in 'depersonalised' or negative feelings towards others and a reduced sense of personal achievement. The people who are most prone to burnout are social workers, counsellors, therapists, spiritual directors, doctors, nurses, chaplains and clergymen of all kinds. In my experience 'burnout' can afflict anyone, e.g. housewives, journalists, broadcasters, police, dentists, pilots, etc.

Gerry Edelwich says that there are five stages to the disillusionment that are characteristic of burnout.

- The first refers to the one that precedes the person's problems and is, therefore, not really a form of burnout. There is *initial enthusiasm.* It is a period of high hopes and lots of energy. The person may be relying too much on ego strength, and not enough on the energy that flows from the deeper self, in order to achieve personal goals. Usually the person is unrealistic in his or her expectations. It is this very idealism that leads him or her to become a helper in the first place.

- The second stage is one of *stagnation.* It is the point where the person's initial enthusiasm begins to fade. The job is no longer the be-all and end-all it once was. The person is not as generous and as empathic as s/he once was. There is a feeling of vague guilt about this together with a concomitant loss of self-esteem.

- The third stage is one of *frustration.* The person not only begins to question his or her professional effectiveness but also the worth-whileness of this particular form of helping.

- The fourth stage is reached when the person retreats into *apathy.* At this point the caring person focuses on facts rather than feelings by offering clinical, dispassionate advice rather than emotional rapport and understanding.

- The fifth and final stage of disillusionment is reached when the person realises what is happening and *intervenes,* often with the help of others, in order to bring the downward cycle to an end, e.g. by means of the creation of an outside life, which involves family, friends, hobbies and other activities.

Three types of role are associated with the different degrees of burnout:

1. Role conflict: A person who has conflicting responsibilities will begin to feel pulled in many directions and will try to do everything equally well without setting priorities. The result will be a feeling of fatigue or exhaustion associated with burnout.

2. Role ambiguity: The individual does not know what is expected of him or her. S/he knows s/he is expected to be a good and effective worker, but is not quite sure how to accomplish this because s/he has no role model or guidelines to follow. The result is that s/he never feels that s/he has accomplished anything worthwhile.

3. Role overload: The individual cannot say 'no' and keeps taking on more responsibility than s/he can handle until s/he finally burns out.

According to psychologists, burnout has three degrees of severity. The first degree is common. There are relatively mild symptoms that can be observed by others and by the sufferer. Warning signs include an inability to shake off a lingering cold, frequent headaches and sleeplessness. First degree burnout is often experienced quite early in one's career. That said, the person continues to work without much sign of trouble. However the thought of going to work may have lost the appeal that that it once had. This kind of burnout can be reversed by things such as taking a short break, a holiday, doing relaxation exercises, or pursuing leisure activities.

The second degree of burnout occurs when the symptoms of the first stage consolidate and get worse. The person suffers from fatigue, prolonged headaches, angry outbursts, irritability and impatience. S/he worries too much about problems and may treat other people badly. For example, somebody who is normally polite and considerate ends up shouting at his or her colleagues. At this stage, job-performance begins to suffer. The person becomes more detached and impersonal while saying 'It's not that I don't want to help, I can't'. Paradoxically, instead of taking things easier, typical sufferers take on extra work. There are two possible reasons for this: a fear of failure, and a reluctance to be inactive and alone because so many painful, negative feelings surface within. But in spite of all their extra efforts they actually accomplish less while reinforcing their stress. Sufferers at this stage can suffer from mistrust, suspicion and mild paranoia.

The third degree of burnout, which is sometimes referred to as 'terminal burnout', occurs when the symptoms mentioned already become chronic. All kinds of crises occur. For example, it can lead to marriage breakdown, or an inability to carry out one's work, and deep questioning. At this stage the person is unable to function normally. Negative feelings such as anxiety, anger, depression, and hostility effect the man or woman's relationships. Physical sickness is common, e.g. heart-attacks or high blood-pressure. Psychological difficulties are also to be expected, e.g. feelings of extreme loneliness and isolation, together with suicidal inclinations. Although third-degree burnout resembles a nervous breakdown, in many regards it is not a genuine one. Rather, it is a case of emotional and physical exhaustion.

A CASE STUDY

Fr Paddy Howell, a Redemptorist, has described a typical experience of burnout in *Family Matters* magazine (no. 5). He had been a member of a school retreat team for 14 years. He realised that he was suffering from terminal burnout when he was extremely upset to hear that a friend of his was planning to leave the country. His disproportionate, over-the-top response was the first inkling he had that something was really wrong. He says that his colleagues were aware that things were not right. 'My burnout symptoms,' he observes, 'included the following: I was depressed and unable to concentrate on the work; I looked awful and felt that I had become an old man within a few days. With neither interest or energy for work I became dependant on a drink or a sleeping tablet to get off to sleep and even then only managed to sleep for a few restless hours.... I dragged myself through each school retreat day, but the joy was gone out of my life. I desperately needed somebody to talk to. I attempted to talk to colleagues. They appeared to be too busy or didn't understand, or simply didn't want to get involved. I was sinking deeper and deeper into depression. Loneliness was gnawing at me. I knew I needed help very badly but I didn't know where to turn.' Eventually Paddy spoke to his GP who in turn referred him to a specialist. After a brief examination he said to him, 'You have been in the front lines for too long and are totally exhausted.' He encouraged Paddy to take a sabbatical. So at the age of 44 he went to the United States for a year. He was away from the demands of work. He was in the company of people who were at the same stage of life as himself and he had more time to study and to pray. During this period of recovery Paddy recognised some of the causes of his burnout. There were unresolved childhood issues. His workload had become too heavy. He hadn't taken proper care of himself. For example, he hadn't budgeted enough time for relaxation, friends and reflection. He had also being trying to take care of elderly parents. As he says, he could have coped with one or two of these issues but not with all of them together at the same time. In retrospect he can see that in many ways his terminal exhaustion proved to be a blessing in disguise in so far as it led to a reordering of his life in the light of new priorities. That is a common experience. However, it is worth noting that it takes a long time to truly recover from third degree burnout. If you wish to do a burnout test on the internet you will find a free one at: *www.queendom.com/tests/career/burnout1.html* It is evaluated online. It consists of 35 questions and takes 15-20 minutes to complete.

Spiritual Effects of Chronic Stress

The experience of burnout occurs when the symptoms become chronic. At this stage the person is unable to function normally. Physical sickness is common and. psychological difficulties are to be expected. The secular self is also threatened. It has a number of characteristics. Its sense of worth is secretly dependent on such things as material possessions, success, reputation and status. It has a compulsive desire to acquire and defend these things, and a lurking fear of losing them. It tends to reject any experience from the outer or inner world that might threaten its sense of security, control and priorities.

During the kind of transitional crises we have already mentioned the things that have been supporting the secular self are removed. Instead of enjoying success, status and a good reputation, a person may have to drink the bitter wine of failure, loss and humiliation. The embattled victim will put up stiff resistance to this process. That can explain why s/he works frantically to retain the very things his or her secular self needs for a sense of well-being. As s/he loses the struggle, the sufferer is filled with fear, anger and hurt. Often these feelings are repressed in a way that creates a lot of tension and strain. As this dynamic predominates, the secular self begins to run out of energy. It begins to suffer from a deep-seated exhaustion or burnout as we have already seen. The joy and peace of the past gives way to spiritual desolation. Feelings of restlessness, agitation, hopelessness and sadness take hold.

As a result, the Lord seems distant and unreal. Prayer is often abandoned or becomes formal. The person goes through the motions, but his or her heart is no longer in it. Spiritual things hold little or no attraction, while the things of the world and the flesh seem very attractive. Temptation is strong and weakness common.

When it hits rock bottom, the personality can hit the 'Rock of Ages'. This happens in two stages. Firstly, the person feels a heartfelt desire for a new experience of God. Secondly, the Lord answers this desire by revealing the length and breadth, the height and depth of the divine love for the person. This kind of religious experience of unconditional, un-merited love can have the effect of refocusing the personality. It begins to move away from false, worldly values, to become more centred on Christ and his gospel. In this way St Paul's advice is fulfilled: 'You must give up your old way of life. You must put aside your old self, which gets corrupted by following illusory desires.' (It is this old self that suffers from stress and burnout.) 'Your mind must be renewed by a spiritual revolution so that you can put on the new self that has been created in God's way' (Eph 4:22-23). I should point out in passing that stress and desolation of spirit are not necessarily synonymous. Many people turn to the Lord with renewed energy during times of strain, seeking God's help. In cases like this, stress can be seen as a providential opportunity of developing an even deeper relationship with the Lord.

Reducing Stress
by Means of Relaxation Exercises

Perhaps the most helpful thing a person can do to reduce stress is to use a relaxation exercise. There are many of them. We will look at a number examples that I have found helpful – physical exercises, belly breathing, Benson's relaxation response, Schultz's autogenic training and Sandford's serenity exercise.

PHYSICAL EXERCISES

Sit or lie quietly. Close your eyes. Clench your fists for about 15 seconds. Then relax them and feel the tension draining away from your arms and muscles. Repeat this twice. Then hunch your shoulders for 15 seconds and relax. Feel the tension draining away. Continue the same method with jaw clenching and relaxing. And finally screw your eyes up tightly and relax them while feeling the tension fading away. Do the same with your legs, and so on.

In his helpful book *QR: The Quieting Reflex* (1983) Charles Stroebel proposes the following exercise:

1. Smile inwardly and then outwardly with your eyes and mouth.

2. Say to yourself mentally in an auto-suggestive way: 'Alert, amused mind; calm body.'

3. Take an easy deep breath.

4. While exhaling your breath, let your jaw, tongue, and shoulders go limp; feel a wave of heaviness come over your limbs and muscles; and feel warmth flowing through your body from head to toes. In a special way imagine warmth flowing into your hands.

5. Resume relaxed, productive living.

BELLY BREATHING

James Gordon of the Center for Mind and Body Medicine in Washington DC maintains that the simplest and perhaps the most effective way of controlling stress is slow, deep breathing. He maintains that whereas babies breathe from their tummies, adults tend to keep their tummies in and breathe from their chests. As a result he advocates belly breathing. He says: 'When you bring air down into the lower portion of the lungs, where oxygen exchange is most efficient, everything changes. Heart rate slows, blood pressure decreases, muscles relax and the mind calms.' Dr Andrew Weil of the University of Arizona endorses this point: 'I have seen breath control alone achieve remarkable results: lowering blood pressure, improving long-standing patterns of poor digestion, allowing people to stop using addictive anti-anxiety drugs and improving sleep and energy cycles.' Experts of this kind suggest the following exercises.

1. Lie on your bed and place a book on your tummy. Relax your stomach muscles and inhale deeply into your belly so that you can see the book rising. When you breathe out, the book should fall. You'll still be bringing oxygen into your upper lungs, but now you are also bringing air deep down into the lower portion of your lungs and expanding your entire chest cavity.

2. Sit upright and place your right hand on your stomach and your left hand on your chest. Breathe deeply so that your right tummy

hand rises and falls with your breath, while your left chest hand stays relatively stationary. Breathe in through your nose and out through your nose or mouth, and enjoy the sensation of belly breathing.

3. Look at the second hand of a clock. Otherwise mentally count cuckoo one, cuckoo two, cuckoo three, etc., on five occasions. Breathe in slowly, filling your tummy for five seconds. Then breathe out slowly for another five seconds.

4. Perform deep belly breathing throughout the day; for example, when you wake up, before you go to sleep and in any stressful situation. Dr Ronald Ley of the University at Albany, New York, is the leading internationally recognised proponent of the notion that hyperventilation contributes to panic attacks. One way of preventing or lessening such attacks is to learn to practice belly breathing.

There is a simpler breathing exercise which goes as follows. Sit or lie quietly. Close your eyes. Imagine a tranquil scene, for example, cotton wool clouds in a blue sky on a summer's day. Breathe slowly and deeply through your nose. Make each out-breath long and soft and steady. Sense the tension leave your body as you exhale. Do this a number of times.

THE RELAXATION RESPONSE

Dr Herbert Benson was a professor of medicine at Harvard Medical School. His main interest was in high blood-pressure, which is often stress-related. He heard that experts in Transcendental Meditation (TM) had claimed that they could influence their autonomic functions such as heart rate and blood pressure. Benson thought that this was highly unlikely because the autonomic system is self governing and, by all accounts, beyond the influence of mind or will. However, he invited some of these experts in TM to participate in clinical trials that could put their claims to the test. In the event, he was surprised to find that they could indeed lower their blood-pressure without the use of drugs.

Benson analysed the TM technique. Having stripped it of its Hindu content, he found he could produce a secular version. It all depended on concentration. During times of stress the mind flits restlessly from one thing to another. It cannot focus on any single item for long. So TM tries to bring about tranquillity by encouraging meditation in a concentrated way on a meaningless word or mantra. Benson wondered if it would not be better to use a word or phrase that would express the person' s faith. He had a medical motive for this, based on the 'placebo effect'. Simply stated, it refers to bodily changes produced by beliefs and expectations. As Benson writes: 'We know that any treatment is more likely to be successful if the patient has a great deal of faith in his physician's ability – or even faith that a higher spiritual power is at work in the body.' As a Christian, I believe that there is such a higher power at work within the human body; we call it the Holy Spirit. Further, I am convinced that when a person receives the Spirit in baptism, s/he also receives the peace and harmony of God. As a result I am sure that this peace is within us at all times, even when we are experiencing stress. It is like a treasure buried in the field of the heart. Therefore I can say without hesitation: 'The peace I want is within'. This phrase expresses my faith.

In his book *Beyond the Relaxation Response* (1985) Benson says that the placebo effect is mobilised by using such a phrase as part of the secularised TM technique. Together they form the 'relaxation response', which can be outlined as follows:

1. Sit in a comfortable position.

2. Close your eyes, smile inwardly and relax your muscles.

3. Focus on your breathing. Breathe slowly and naturally.

4. Select a word or phase that expresses your faith conviction, for example 'maranatha' (which in Aramaic means 'Come Lord Jesus') or 'The peace I want is within.' This latter phrase is the ideal length for a mantra because it is seven syllables long. This word or phrase is repeated slowly on each outward breath. The key to the exercise is to try to think of nothing other than the words you are saying to yourself. In this connection Benson quotes the *Catholic Encyclopaedia* with approval: ' Attention is the very essence of prayer; as soon as this attention ceases, prayer ceases.'

5. When distracting thoughts intrude and upset your attention, disregard them gently by saying something like: 'Oh well.' Then quietly return to the word or phrase you are using. It is essential to maintain a passive relaxed attitude in dealing with any interruptions. Do not try to force yourself to attend. This will only make you tense and anxious about not succeeding. If this exercise is followed for twenty minutes a day, two things will happen. First, you will get used to using it. Second, it will have a very calming effect.

The exercise that Benson recommends is very similar to the form of prayer advocated by John Cassian (360-433). He suggested that those who wanted to pray without ceasing should repeat the verse, 'O Lord come to my assistance, O Lord make haste to help me' (Ps 70:1). In the Middle Ages, the anonymous author of *The Cloud of Unknowing,* encouraged people to repeat a single word rather than a phrase, such as 'God' or 'love'. In the nineteenth century the unknown Russian author of *The Way of the Pilgrim* discovered that he could pray unceasingly by repeating the traditional Jesus Prayer, 'Lord Jesus Christ, have mercy on me.' In the twentieth century, a number of spiritual guides, such as John Main and Basil Pennington have revived the use of mantras in what is known as centring prayer. So there is no need to be wary of Benson's exercise even if he was inspired by Transcendental Meditation. A similar form of prayer has been influential in the Christian Church for many centuries.

A Peripheral Vision Exercise

Sit down and look at the wall opposite you but a little above eye level. Continue to look at this point in soft focus throughout this exercise. After a while you may find that as you concentrate on this point the rest of the room goes a little vague or fuzzy and you develop a kind of tunnel vision. We utilise this kind of tunnel vision a lot nowadays, for example watching television and working with computers. We only see the screen. Again when we are reading or writing we have to focus our vision in a very specific way. Even when we talk to someone we are inclined to focus our vision on their mouth and eyes rather than the rest of them. This kind of focused visual attention can have an effect on the way we perceive the world so that we get fixated on activities and things. This kind of thinking can be associated with worry, adrenaline, and stress.

But there is another way of looking at the environment. You can experience it as you look at the specific point on the wall. Begin to broaden your field of vision and notice more and more of what's on either side of that point, so that soon you are paying attention to what you can see out of the corners of your eyes on each side. And you can take your awareness even further by going out as far as you can to the left and right. As you stay in peripheral vision, you may notice that your breathing has moved lower down in your chest and maybe slowed down or become deeper, that the muscles of your face and jaw have relaxed. Perhaps it is too soon for this to have happened yet, but if you were to stay in peripheral vision for any length of time, you might find your hands beginning to get warm, or even your feet.

The interesting thing is that when you go into peripheral vision you seem to activate the parasympathetic nervous system; the part that calms you down, and slows you down, and lets your mind and body and emotions come back into balance. So begin to do this while letting your field of vision return to normal.

Nowadays there are strange computer generated pictures that help one to relax. When a person looks at them they seem to have no apparent image within them. However if you let your attention to relax by focusing on the surface of the picture the brain begins to perceive hidden shapes within it. It is a truly magical experience when a seemingly chaotic and meaningless picture suddenly reveals hidden three-dimensional images within itself. For example, an American company has published three books entitled *Magic Eye,* each of which contains optical illusions of this kind. As one focuses on the images in an undistracted way they can have a relaxing effect, not only upon the mind, but on the body as well.

AUTOGENIC TRAINING

Dr Johannes Schultz pioneered autogenic training as a means of relaxation in the 1920s. Over the years it has been perfected by other researchers, notably Dr Wolfgang Luthe. This method uses verbal cues to influence the autonomic system in order to produce deep relaxation. It is similar in many ways to the relaxation response in which one focuses attention on a word or phrase. In contrast, autogenic training focuses attention on physical sensations. So the key to this form of exercise is a form of auto-suggestion called 'passive concentration'. It affirms that different parts of the body are getting heavy and warm. I often use it.

First, I try to become aware of the sensations in my feet, noticing whether they are warm or cold, tense or relaxed. Then I imagine that they are getting heavy and warm. After a while I usually begin to sense the warmth. I focus my attention on that sensation and affirm that it is getting stronger. This is not done by a determined act of will. On the contrary it is a matter of believing that the gift of warmth is there to be discovered, so to speak. Having spent some time on my feet I might move to my hands and arms in a similar way. As I go through the exercise I can sense the tension leaving my muscles and a lovely feeling of relaxation spreading through my body. Here is a brief outline of the method.

1. *Deep breathing exercises*
(a) Imagine ocean waves rolling in ... and out.
(b) Silently say to yourself: 'My breathing is smooth and rhythmic.'

2. *Heartbeat regulation exercises*
(a) Imagine ocean waves.
(b) Silently say: 'My heartbeat is slow and regular.'

3. *Blood flow*
(a) Right arm and hand
      Silently say: 'My right arm and hand are heavy and warm'
      Imagine the warm sun shining on them.
(b) Left arm and hand
      Silently say: 'My left arm and hand are heavy and warm.'
      Imagine the warm sun shining on them.
(c) Legs and feet
      Silently say: 'My legs and feet are heavy and warm.'
      Imagine the warmth flowing down from the arms and into the
      hands.

4. *Summing up phrase*
'I am calm'

5. *Return to activity*
Move again from step one to step three.

A SERENITY EXERCISE

Mrs Agnes Sanford was a pioneer in the rediscovery of the ministry of
healing. In 1949 she published a book, *The Healing Light*, which has
since become a classic. In it she describes a prayer exercise that I have
adapted slightly.

1.   Lay aside your cares and worries as best you can. Quieten your
      mind and concentrate on the reality of God. You may not know

the Lord in a personal way. But you know that something sustains the universe. That something is not ourselves. So the first step is to remind yourself that there is a source of life outside yourself.

2. The second step is to get in touch with the source of life by saying a prayer like this: 'Heavenly Father, please increase in me at this time your life-giving power.' If you do not know this outside life as your heavenly Father, you could simply say: 'Whoever you are, whatever you are, come into me now.'

3. The third step is to *believe* and *affirm* that the power is coming into you. Recall what Jesus promised: 'Whatever you ask for in prayer, believing you have it already, it will be yours' (Mk 11:24). Accept the power in faith. No matter how much you ask for something, it only becomes yours as you *accept* it and give thanks for it. 'Thank you,' you can say, 'that your life is *now* coming into me and increasing life in my body, mind and spirit.'

4. The fourth step is to *observe* the operations of that life. In order to do this, you must decide on some tangible thing that you wish to be accomplished by that power, for example, a decrease in stress and an increase of inner peace. You could say something like this: 'I thank you Lord, that the relaxation and peace I desire is being revealed within me, by the light of your Spirit.'

As we come to the end of this section, here is another recommendation. Nowadays you can buy relaxation tapes in many shops. As you play the tape or CD you follow the instructions of the speaker. A man who uses one, last thing at night, told me that he never heard the end of it, because he always fell asleep first. Listening to certain types of music can also be relaxing. There are many studies demonstrating how mellifluous forms of music can evoke relaxing physiological responses, including changes in breathing, heart-rate, blood-pressure, blood-supply and galvanic skin responses. Some classical music is ideal for the purpose, e.g. Bach's *Concerto for Two*

Violins, Allegri's *Miserere,* or Barber's *Adagio for Strings.* The bigger record stores also sell CDs with collections of tranquil tracks.

LAUGHTER THE BEST MEDICINE

For many years the *Reader's Digest* has included a section entitled: 'Laughter the best Medicine'. There are good religious and medical reasons for maintaining this. In Proverbs 17:22 we read: 'A cheerful heart is a good medicine, but a downcast spirit dries up the bones.' Since time immemorial, sages and doctors alike have advocated a merry heart as a perfect remedy for life's vicissitudes. For instance, the Greek poet Pindar wrote: 'The best healer is good cheer', and the poet Longfellow wrote: 'Joy, temperance and repose, slam the door on the doctor's nose.' It is not surprising therefore that modern medical research should discover that laughter is therapeutic. Its effect on the heart is rather akin to a vigorous massage. During laughter, the heart beat quickens and blood pressure rises; after laughter, however, both heart rate and blood pressure drop to a point that is lower than its initial resting state.

The repeated research experiments of Dr Lee Berk at Loma Linda University School of Medicine, California, shows that laughter, happiness and joy 'inspire' the immune system to create white 'T' cells, commonly called 'happy cells', which help to prevent infection. The philosopher Friedrich Nietzche hit upon the idea of joyful immunity when he wrote: 'Contentment preserves one even from catching cold.' Dr Berk's research work has also found that the 'mirthful laughter experience' as he calls it, appears to reduce the high levels of cortisol, dopac, adrenaline and growth hormone which are brought about by high levels of tension, thereby creating a reverse effect to the classical hormone response during times of stress. Both physically and psychologically, it is as if laughter acts as a 'safety valve' for the discharge of nervous energy. The psychologist and mystic Alan Watts once wrote: 'The whole art of life is in knowing how to transform anxiety into laughter.' Irish writer C.S. Lewis observed that laughter was the vocalisation of inner health. So if you are feeling up-tight why not try enjoying a comedian, situation comedy or an amusing movie on TV. If you watch the likes of Basil in *Fawlty Towers*, or Victor Meldrew in *One Foot in the Grave* you will be sure to smile and laugh, thereby reducing tension. Here is an account of an Irish bricklayer's insurance claim. It describes a very stressful situation. See if it makes you smile.

Dear Sir,

I am writing in response to your request for additional information in block number 3 of the accident reporting form. I put 'Poor Planning' as the cause of my accident. You asked for a fuller explanation and I trust the following details will be sufficient.

I am a bricklayer by trade. On the day of the accident, I was working alone on the roof of a new six-story building. When I completed my work, I found I had some bricks left over which, when weighed later, were found to weigh 240 lbs. Rather than carry the bricks down by hand, I decided to lower them in a barrel by using a pulley which was attached to the side of the building at the sixth floor. Securing the rope at ground level, I went up to the roof, swung the barrel out and loaded the bricks into it. Then I went down and untied the rope, holding it tightly to insure a slow descent for the 240 lbs of bricks. You will note on the accident reporting form that my weight is 135 lbs.

Due to my surprise at being jerked off the ground so suddenly, I lost my presence of mind and forgot to let go of the rope. Needless to say, I proceeded at a rapid rate up the side of the building. In the vicinity of the third floor, I met the barrel which was now proceeding downward at an equally impressive speed. This explains the fractured skull, minor abrasions and the broken collarbone, as listed in Section 3 of the accident reporting form. Slowed only slightly, I continued my rapid ascent, not stopping until the fingers of my right hand were two knuckles deep into the pulley which I mentioned in

Paragraph 2 of this correspondence. Fortunately by this time I had regained my presence of mind and was able to hold tightly to the rope, in spite of the excruciating pain I was now beginning to experience.

At approximately the same time, however, the barrel of bricks hit the ground, and the bottom fell out of the barrel. Now devoid of the weight of the bricks, the barrel weighed approximately 50 lbs. I refer you again to my weight. As you might imagine, I began a rapid descent down the side of the building. In the vicinity of the third floor, I met the barrel coming up. This accounts for the two fractured ankles, broken tooth and severe lacerations of my legs and lower body. Here my luck began to change slightly. The encounter with the barrel seemed to slow me enough to lessen my injuries when I fell into the pile of bricks and fortunately only three vertebrae were cracked.

I am sorry to report, however, as I lay there on the pile of bricks, in pain, unable to move and watching the empty barrel six stories above me, I again lost my composure and presence of mind and let go of the rope…

Reducing Stress
by Means of Changes in Lifestyle

In 1943 Reinhold Niebuhr wrote the following prayer: 'God give us the grace to accept with serenity the things that cannot be changed, courage to change the things which should be changed, and the wisdom to distinguish one from the other.' The experience of chronic stress is an invitation to change the aspects of our lifestyle that contribute to it. They can and should be changed.

ESTABLISH PRIORITIES

It is important to discriminate between needs and priorities. Otherwise you will be swamped by an endless succession of urgent needs. A few years ago I had a chat with Seán, a curate in a Dublin parish. 'What are your priorities from a personal point of view?' I asked. 'I must admit,' he replied, 'that I haven't given the thing much thought.' 'As you think about it now,' I said, 'what would you like your top priority to be?' Sean reflected for a while, then he said: 'I think that parish visitation should be my number one priority.' 'Well, do you get much time to visit?' I asked. 'Frankly, no,' Sean replied, 'other things seem to demand my attention. For example last night I had to attend a committee meeting. Tonight I'm judging a beauty competition in a local hotel. It's like that all the time.' 'But if pastoral visitation is a priority,' I retorted, 'wouldn't it be better to say "no" to the many invitations you receive. You would feel that you are doing something really worthwhile, instead of feeling guilty about not visiting.' The curate was no different from countless other people. Because he had failed to discriminate between needs and priorities he was hassled in a stressful way by countless demands on his time.

We begin to take control of our lives when we begin to establish long-term and short-term goals, i.e. for the following year and the following day. Having made a list of between five and ten long-term goals, try to number them in their order of importance: 1, 2, 3, etc. Then try to work out a practical plan that indicates what has to be done and when. It is much the same when it comes to short-term goals for the following day. I read an interesting story in this connection. The president of an American steel company went to a New York consultant. 'I'll pay you any price,' he said, 'if you will tell me how to get more things done without undue stress.' The consultant replied: 'At night spend five minutes analysing your problems of the following day. Write them down on a sheet of paper, but place them in their order of importance. Then tackle the first item as soon as you get to the office. Stick to it until it is finished. Then move to the number two and so on. Test this method as long as you like, and then send me what you think it is worth.'

Some time later the consultant received a note from the company president. Enclosed was a check for $25,000 with the words, 'For the most helpful advice I ever received.' Evidently the New York consultant knew about the Pareto Principle, or the 80/20 rule. It states that if a person has listed ten goals in their order of importance, and tackles the top two, eighty per cent of his potential effectiveness will be derived from them. Only twenty per cent of his effectiveness will be derived from the other eight! People who fail to discriminate between top priorities and lesser ones, can end up using a lot of energy achieving very little. So time management is really worthwhile. It increases efficiency, while protecting the person from the tyranny of having to respond to endless needs. In the name of worthwhile priorities we can say 'no' with a good conscience. Instead of life controlling us, we can learn to regain control of our lives. As we do so, our stress levels will fall.

EXERCISE AND DIET

When we looked at chronic stress we saw that feelings of distress are due to the fact that our bodies are reacting to excessive levels of adrenaline and other substances. What is needed is some way of reducing those levels. Our ancestors would have done this by means of vigorous 'flight or fight', but we can have the same effect by taking exercise. It helps us to use up our surplus energy so that we feel more relaxed afterwards. Not only that, exercise helps us to become fit and contributes to our sense of well-being. There is also evidence to show that exercise enables the body to secrete chemicals that help to produce a state of physical harmony. Knowing this to be true, one American professor of psychology refuses to see stressful or depressed clients unless they are willing to take an hour's walk every day. So why not plan to take some form of regular exercise such as swimming, jogging or golf. It is important that you enjoy the exercise and that you set realistic goals for yourself. Otherwise you will not keep it up. For example, walking is an excellent form of exercise. You could plan to take a half-hour walk five days a week. It needs to be energetic enough to stimulate the heart to greater efforts.

Besides taking exercise, diet too can help to control tension. First, it is important to avoid taking chemicals that increase stress, e.g. caffeine, tannin, salt, nicotine, sugar and the like. In many cases substitutes like decaffeinated coffee and artificial sugars can be used. Where this is not possible moderation is the key to success. Here are some tips that the experts suggest.

- Eat three meals a day, especially breakfast.
- Take a vitamin supplement; be sure to get enough vitamin C and calcium by drinking orange juice and milk.
- Eat more fibre – it reduces cholesterol levels that may have been elevated by stress.
- Limit your intake of cholesterols and saturated fats. For example, there are butter substitutes, such as Benecol, which can reduce harmful (LDL) cholesterol levels. The same company also

produces yogurts, and cheeses. These products incorporate plant stanolesters that block absorption of cholesterol from the intestine.

- Eat carbohydrates – they release a sleep-inducing chemical called serotonin.
- If you are over-weight try to plan a sensible diet. In other words, do it slowly. As you lose surplus pounds you will feel better physically and emotionally. Your stress levels will go down, while your self-esteem will go up.

THE IMPORTANCE OF LEISURE

People suffering from stress often complain about all the work they *have* to do. Yet when they could take time off, they avoid doing so because they would be unable to relax and face themselves. As a result they tend to take on more work, thereby reinforcing their stress. The only way to break out of this vicious circle is to *decide* to take time off for recreation. This can be done in three ways, in personal reflection, sharing with friends, and pursuing hobbies.

Self-awareness
It is refreshing to spend time with oneself, becoming aware of what is going on within. St Augustine wrote in his *Confessions:* 'Men go abroad to admire the heights and mountains, the mighty billows of the sea, the long courses of rivers, the vast extent of the ocean, the circular motion of the stars, and yet pass themselves by.' There is a story in the life of Dr Carl Jung that illustrates the importance of this kind of self-intimacy. Apparently a society lady phoned him to request an urgent appointment at 3 p.m. the following Thursday. Jung said it would not be possible because he already had an important appointment at that very time. Well, on the Thursday the same lady happened to sail past Jung's garden which ran down to the shores of Lake Zurich. There was the famous doctor, his shoes off, sitting on a wall, his feet dangling in the water. As soon as she got home the irate

woman rang Jung demanding an explanation. 'You told me,' she exclaimed, 'that you couldn't see me because you had an important appointment. Nevertheless I saw you at that very hour, whiling away the time at the bottom of your garden.' 'I told you no lie,' the doctor replied, 'I had an appointment at that time, the most important of the week, an appointment with myself.'

The purpose of time on one's own is fivefold.

- Firstly, I listen to my own experience in order to *recover* my feelings which can often lurk unrecognised in the twilight zone of pre-consciousness.
- Secondly, I try to *name* my feelings. Instead of saying 'I feel good or bad about the invitation to the wedding', I try to be more specific about what I feel, e.g. 'I feel delighted', or 'surprised' or 'scared' by the invitation.
- Thirdly, I try to *own* my feelings, rather than thinking about them, or analysing them in a detached, dispassionate way. For example it would mean that instead of saying with a smile, 'I seem to have a lot of anger within me' I would say with a frown, 'I am very angry, because I feel hurt and humiliated.'
- Fourthly, I try to *understand* my feelings to see where they are coming from. As John Powell once wrote: 'Other people can stimulate my emotions, but the *causes* lie within.' What perceptions, values, beliefs, or memories evoked such feelings. Have they their roots in the distant past, especially in childhood? For example, perhaps I was intimidated by a person in authority yesterday, and had an exaggerated desire to please him or her, but was disappointed and upset when s/he took very little notice of me. Could such a reaction be traced back to an overweening desire to impress one's parents in childhood in order to win their affection? Are such perceptions realistic now that I am an adult?
- Fifthly, it is good to *express* one's feelings, to a friend in conversation, and to God in prayer. Once I become aware of what is going on within me, and why, all sorts of issues can be faced and sorted out in a way that reduces stress.

Friendship

Spending time with friends is also important. Our work requires us to fulfil all kinds of roles and to keep our thoughts and feelings to ourselves, especially when they are negative ones. It is great when we can share them with someone who is prepared to listen with empathy and understanding. We can let off steam with friends in the knowledge that they will accept and love us as we are, and not as we pretend to be. This kind of mutual communication can have a very soothing, therapeutic effect, especially for natural extroverts. Often they only discover what they are thinking and feeling as they talk. Otherwise they become frustrated, lonely and stressful. As English writer Francis Bacon said: 'The man or woman without friends becomes the cannibal of his or her own heart.'

Scripture values the protective and therapeutic effects of friendship. For instance, we read: 'Two are better than one, because they have a good return for their work: If one falls down, his friend can help him up. But pity the man who falls and has no one to help him up! Also, if two lie down together, they will keep warm. But how can one keep warm alone? Though one may be overpowered, two can defend themselves. A cord of three strands is not quickly broken' (Eccl 4:9-12). In Sir 6:14-17 we read: 'A faithful friend is a sturdy shelter: he that has found one has found a treasure. There is nothing so precious as a faithful friend, and no scales can measure his excellence. A faithful friend is an elixir of life; and those who fear the Lord will find him. Whoever fears the Lord directs his friendship aright, for as he is, so is his neighbour also.'

Hobbies

The pursuit of a hobby, such as music-making, painting, bird-watching, stamp collecting, fishing, embroidery, or woodwork, can be relaxing and enjoyable. As the psalmist says: 'I will solve my riddle to the music of the harp' (Ps 49:4). It is important to plan for leisure time. Unless this is a personal priority, it will be sacrificed in order to respond to all kinds of needs. The Comte de Mirabeau had the right idea when he wrote: 'I would not exchange my leisure hours for all the wealth in the world.' In my experience many people feel guilty about 'wasting time' on hobbies. Perhaps this reaction is rooted in the unconscious assumption of the work ethic, that a person is only lovable for what s/he does and not for who s/he is.

Meditation
There are forms of meditation like TM and the use of Christian mantras that have a proven ability, when properly used, to bring about tranquillity of mind and body. Apparently they can help the brain's *alpha* rhythms, which are characteristic of the waking state, change to the *beta* rhythms, which are characteristic of the sleeping state. But I have found that when Christians engage in conventional forms of prayerful meditation such as the Benedictine *Lectio Divina,* or Ignatian forms of imaginative reflection, they too have a calming effect. These and other useful methods of prayer are contained in Anthony de Mello's classic book, *Sadhana: A Way to God.*

An article entitled 'Religious Orientation and Psychological Well-being: The Role of the Frequency of Personal Prayer' in the *British Journal of Health Psychology* (No. 4, 1999) examined the effects of what Gordon Allport referred to as intrinsic religion on mental health. People who have intrinsic, as opposed to extrinsic religion, are those who have internalised their faith in such a way that it influences every aspect of their everyday lives. They spend time in regular prayer of a personal, God-centred variety. Consequently, they are more inclined to have a joyful sense of ultimate belonging, a conviction that one is simultaneously connected to a loving God, the universe and one's deepest self. Research shows that this kind of prayer is an effective antidote to the anxious alienation that is so characteristic of Western societies. For more on the important topic of prayerful meditation and inner peace see my *Prayer in Practice: A Biblical Approach* (Dublin: Columba, 2000).

Reducing Stress
by Changing Attitudes

Earlier it was stated that stress depends on a person's reactions, and not on outside events, e.g. having to give a talk in public could cause great stress in one person and none in another. The reason for the difference is psychological. Our reactions are rooted in our attitudes and beliefs, many of which can be unrealistic and unreasonable. In this section we are going to look at three such examples.

IRRATIONAL BELIEFS

A well known psychologist called Ellis has suggested that our feelings about events are predetermined by our beliefs and perception. As a result he talks about the ABC of emotions. It can be outlined as follows:

A   refers to the *activating event*, e.g. being licked on the face by a big dog.

B   refers to *beliefs* about the events, for example:
   - 'The dog likes me'
   - 'Dogs can bite you for no apparent reason'
   - 'Dogs are lovely cuddly creatures'
   - 'Dogs are man's best friends, loyal and true'

C   refers to *consequent feelings*, ones that follow from one's belief about the event. For example, the person who believes that dogs are unhygienic or liable to attack is going to feel fear, while the person who thinks that they are cuddly and loyal is going to feel attraction and love.

Ellis maintained that a lot of stressful, negative feelings, are due to the fact that our beliefs about the world are both unrealistic and unreasonable. He thought that stress could be reduced if and when irrational beliefs and perceptions were recognised and changed. He and his followers have listed many of the common ones. I will mention nine of them. See if any apply to you. Ask a friend what he or she thinks about your answers.

- I need everyone's love and approval for about everything I do.
- I should be able to do everything well.
- If something bad could, or does happen, I should worry about it.
- It is easier to avoid difficult tasks, than to try them and risk failure.
- I will enjoy life if I avoid responsibilities and take what I get right now.
- A person's worth is directly related to his objectively discernible productivity.
- Anger is automatically bad and destructive, and should always be repressed.
- People are very fragile and one should keep one's thoughts to oneself in order to avoid hurting others.
- Happiness, pleasure, fulfilment and growth can only be achieved in the company of others, never on one's own.

Mastering One's Imagination

Shortly before last Christmas I felt very stressed. One day I was thinking of all the cards I had to write, the presents I had to buy, the trips I had to make, people I needed to contact either by phone or in person, events I needed to organise, new tyres I needed to get for the car, and so on. The thought of so many things that needed doing in such a short period of time caused me to panic. I thought to myself, 'It is impossible. I will never be able to get so many things done in such a short time.' The acute fear I experienced led to a kind of paralysis. I felt so overwhelmed by the sheer impossibility of accomplishing all the tasks that I was unable to do anything at all. It was if I was saying to myself, 'Why start, it is all hopeless!' Then I remembered something that a colleague had told me some years before.

Apparently, he had gone to a barren area of North Africa for a time of prayer and reflection. When he arrived at his destination he was met by a Little Brother of Charles de Foucauld. He told this colleague of mine that he would be on his own for most of his stay. He proffered this advice: 'It is important that you live entirely in the present because that is the moment where God is truly present. Your enemies will be the past and the future. Neither is real. The first, which is over, will try to invade the present moment by means of your memory, while the second, which is yet to come, will try to invade the present moment by means of your imagination. Resist the workings of both memory, which evokes guilt, and imagination, which evokes fear, in order to live in the grace of the present moment.' This point reminded me of something Jesus said: 'Therefore do not worry about tomorrow, for tomorrow will worry about itself. Each day has enough trouble of its own' (Matt 6:34). I also recalled something St Padre Pio prayed: 'Lord, I commend my past to your mercy, my future to your providence, and my present to your love.'

As soon as I recalled all this I tried to rein in my over-active imagination with the bridle and bit of reason and faith. I thought to myself, I'll write down all the things I have to do in their order of importance. Then I will begin to tackle the various tasks, one by one, starting right now. As soon as I disciplined and controlled my imagination, in this way, I felt a new surge of hope and energy. My stress levels went down quickly. I began to carry out the nominated tasks in sequence. By living in the present I found that I wasn't fearful of the future. I got everything done much more quickly and efficiently than I had ever suspected. But I learned a lesson. Stress can be fuelled by an imagination that gets out of hand by picturing all the scary things that might, or might not happen, in the future.

COPING WITH CONFLICT IN A CONSTRUCTIVE WAY

In relationships at home and at work, conflicts are inevitable. Here is list of typical ones:

- Having to say 'no' to a request for help.
- Coping with criticism from another person, e.g. the boss.
- Stating your rights and needs, e.g. in a restaurant.
- Expressing negative feelings such as anger.
- Giving a negative response to someone or having to confront them, e.g. telling a son or daughter they have to be home at midnight, not three in the morning.
- Differing from the majority opinion at a meeting.
- Making a request, e.g. asking a friend for money.
- Initiating social contacts, e.g. at a wedding where you know none of the guests.

There are two stressful and inappropriate ways of coping with conflict. The first, is to be *passive*, to back down because of lack of self-esteem and the belief that one should make peace at any price. For example, one has arranged to meet a friend at 3pm at a well known landmark in the centre of town. She does not turn up till 3.30 and offers no explanation. You feel hurt and angry. But instead of saying anything about your feelings you smile and say nothing.

The second way of coping with a conflict is to become *aggressive* and overbearing. So when the friend turns up late, you attack her verbally in judgmental and critical words: 'You are completely unreliable, your word means nothing. You don't give a damn about anybody.' Granted this is a way of letting off emotional steam. But it is hurtful and will cause a rift between the two people and may evoke a counter-attack. Either way it is likely to increase stress.

The third way of coping is to act *assertively*. When the friend arrives late I express what I feel: 'I felt hurt and angry when you didn't turn up at the time we arranged. I felt let-down and taken for granted.' In this way one lets off steam, but without attacking the other person and so stress levels can be reduced.

This assertiveness can be used in all kinds of situations. For example, you are making a point at a meeting when someone rudely interrupts. You can respond in a constructive way by saying: 'Could you wait a moment, I want to finish my point, it is important to me.' The same approach can be used in a shop where you were sold a defective article. 'The clock you sold me doesn't work correctly. I want a replacement.' If the assistant begins to argue the point, do not get involved, keep on asserting your position: 'The clock doesn't work. I want a new one please!' Many people find it hard to be assertive because of a lack of self-acceptance.

FROM OBLIGATION TO PERSONAL CONVICTION

Many people suffer from what has been called 'hardening of the oughteries'. They are normally motivated by a sense of cheerless obligation, the 'oughts, musts, and have-tos' of other people. As a result, they begin to lose touch with their own deeper desires and inner freedom. Consequently, they may feel that they are losing control of their lives, and are hapless pawns on the chessboard of life. They spend their days trying to please other people, not out of love, but because of fear, and a fear of condemnation or criticism. Needless to say, this is a stressful experience. The way to overcome this sense of suffocation is to get used to asking the question, 'In the light of my beliefs, and values, what do I want in these circumstances?' On getting in touch with what is going on within, you will be in contact with your deeper self and your own creativity and freedom. As a result you will have an increased sense of autonomy and self-determination. You may do many of the same things as before, but for a different motive.

STRUCTURAL CHANGE

Most counsellors and psychotherapists e.g. in the Freudian, Jungian and Rogerian tradition, try get their clients to adapt, in a competent and realistic way, to the world around them. Others maintain, e.g.

Fromm and Marcuse, that we live in an abnormal society. Therefore it is understandable when people develop 'abnormal' reactions to it. But they would argue that if counsellors and psychotherapists focus exclusively on people's conscious and unconscious reactions, while encouraging them to adapt to an abnormal environment, it is a political act. By failing to critique the questionable and often unjust values and mores or modern society, they are conspiring, albeit unwittingly, in the stressful oppression of their clients.

While it is true that the individual person can and indeed should take steps to reduce his or her stress levels, often they will not be fully effective unless there are structural changes as well. As the Irish Health and Safety Authority points out, the traditional approach of using stress management to train individual workers 'to cope' is likely to be ineffective. One could also argue that some doctors are engaged, in an implicit way, in reactionary political activity if and when they help their patients to conform to dysfunctional structures, by giving them tranquillisers. Surely, they should be helping them to question and change the very structures that are causing their stress. Changes, safeguards and controls need to be implemented primarily at an *organisational* level, i.e. at the source of the problem. Employers and managers need to evaluate, with the help of staff feedback, where and how they may be needlessly contributing to the stress of the workforce. This may lead to an acknowledgment of the need for changes in such things as management style, organisation, working conditions, social support, career development and training, staff communication, and so on. Of course, our places of work are part of the wider society. Arguably, there is need for socio-economic reform at a national level, so that there is a greater sense of fairness and respect for human dignity. To make these kind of changes needs both political vision as well as a decision to makes adjustments where they are required. Otherwise many citizens, such as the travelling people and immigrants into Ireland, will continue to experience the kind of discrimination and prejudice that can lead to great stress. It is a normal reaction to an abnormal situation.

Biblical Faith and Peace of Mind

The pace and pressures of modern life can be hectic. Crises of all kinds are common. If we learn to cope in the light of God's willingness to help, we will cope much better. It is simply a matter of *nestling* in the Lord, rather than *wrestling* alone with difficulties. This point of view is illustrated over and over again in the Scriptures. We will examine one example from 2 Chronicles 20 in some detail.

Facing impossible odds
The Jewish King Jehoshaphat received news that his kingdom was about to be attacked by a huge army. From a military point of view the position was hopeless. Not surprisingly, the king was filled with fear and disquiet. But instead of magnifying the problem by focusing his attention on it, he magnified the Lord by focusing on God by means of prayer and fasting.

Hearing God's word and comfort
Having poured out his heart to the Lord, Jehoshaphat waited for a response. It came through one of his priests. Inspired by the Spirit he said: 'Your majesty, and all you people of Judah and Jerusalem, the Lord says you must not be discouraged or afraid to face this large army. The battle depends on God and not on you.' This prophetic word finds an echo many times in the Scriptures. In Exodus 14:14, Moses says: 'Do not be afraid. Stand firm and you will see the deliverance the Lord will bring you today. *The Lord will fight for you, you need only be still.*' Normally we translate Psalm 37:7 as 'Be still and know that I am God'. However, it could be more accurately translated as '*Stop fighting*, and

know that I am God, supreme among the nations.' In other words, when faced with difficulties, trust in the Lord, do what God says and wait for what the Almighty will do on your behalf.

Anticipating victory in praise
Knowing that God would be true to the divine word, King Jehoshaphat worshipped the Lord while his priests praised Yahweh with loud voices. The following morning the king 'appointed men to sing to the Lord and to praise him for the splendour of his holiness as they went out at the head of the army'. This is a typical example of what is known in Hebrew as the *teruwah Yahweh* or 'victory shout'. It was a religious war cry meant to strike terror into enemies and to anticipate the manifestation of God's saving help. For example the 'victory shout' preceded the fall of Jericho. Again on Palm Sunday it anticipated the resurrection of Jesus and his victory over sin, Satan and death. The King and his people believed in the Lord, and as a result they came to see the victory that they had desired, and which God had promised. Their enemies were defeated. The Jews did not have to strike a blow.

THE WAY OF EXPRESSING FAITH IN TIMES OF STRESS

Having reflected on the biblical pattern of faith, we can go on to apply it in our own lives. There are three steps which spell the word THE.

> **T** refers to *Thanking* God no matter what happens
> **H** refers to *Handing* your difficulties to the Lord.
> **E** refers to *Expecting* the Lord to help you.

Let us look at each step in turn

Thanking God in all circumstances
On a number of occasions in the New Testament we are told:
- 'Pray constantly and for *all things* give thanks to the Lord' (1 Thess 5:18).

- '*Always* give thanks for *everything*, to God the Father' (Eph 5:19).
- 'If there is anything you need, pray for it asking God for it with prayer and *thanksgiving*' (Phil 4:6-7)

No matter what pressures and demands we have to face, we should pray with praise and thanksgiving. We do so in the belief that God will bring good out of the negative circumstances of our lives. The notion of the 'happy fault' lies behind this confidence in God's providence. It comes from the Easter liturgy, where the sin of Adam is referred to as a *felix culpa* (i.e. happy fault) – which gained for us so great a Redeemer! St Paul echoed this insight when he wrote that, by turning *everything* to their good, God co-operates with those who love the Lord (Rom 8.28). Having poured out our feelings to God we express our faith conviction to the Father in the form of praise and thanksgiving. In doing so, many of us have found that it opens the heart to the graces God wants to give.

Handing our difficulties to the Lord
In I Peter 57 we read: 'Cast your anxieties on the Lord, for he cares about you.' Anxieties seem to have a gravitational pull that draws our attention away from God to ourselves. As a result many of us seem to cling to our worries and cares. It takes an act of will to reverse this dynamic. We have to make a conscious decision to hand over our lives and our problems into the care of God as we understand God.

Expect the Lord to help you
When we trust the Lord we can be sure that God will comfort us. As Heb 13:5-6 reads: 'God has said, "I will never desert you, nor will I forsake you." The Lord is my helper. I will not be afraid; what can man do to me?' St Paul adds: 'God helps us in all our troubles' (2 Cor 1:4-5). No matter how weak and vulnerable we may feel, 'God's power is made perfect in our weakness' (2 Cor 12:8).

I had a memorable experience of this truth in the mid-eighties. I had been invited to speak at a conference, for Italians in Assisi. When I got to Rome, *en route* to my destination, I was suffering from chronic stress. I was anxious about everything. What would I say at the conference? Would my interpreter be able to cope? Would I be able to find out what buses and trains I would need to get to my engagement? The more I thought about these things, the more my stress increased. I had a blinding headache. My body was like a wound-up spring. Finally, I turned to the Lord. I poured out my feelings, all of them negative. Having tried to thank the Lord, I implored God to help me. After a while I recalled a text in Isaiah 41:10, 'Fear not, I am with you, be not dismayed, for I am your God, I will strengthen you, I will uphold you with my victorious right hand.' I focused on the words 'I will strengthen and uphold you.' That was just what I needed to hear. I asked the Lord to carry out the divine promises. Nothing seemed to happen. I felt very disappointed, and told the Lord so. Then I went back to the verse and noticed that the Lord had said: 'Fear not, be not dismayed.' Perhaps this was not a word of advice, but rather a word of command. So I said to the Lord: 'Be it done unto me according to thy word. If you want me to be courageous I *will* be courageous. I'll take on the whole of Italy if necessary. But first, you must help me.' Well, it was like a miracle. As soon as I said this prayer, a great calm came upon me. My headache disappeared. My tension melted. Stress was replaced by a quiet confidence in the Lord. It never deserted me. I sailed through the conference without a worry. The Lord had been as good as his word.

Accept divine peace
Over a period of time I have come to appreciate the fact that there is a difference between physical relaxation and spiritual peace. Needless to say there is a connection between the two, but it is quite possible that a person would be suffering from stress while being at peace deep down in his or her heart, on account of having a good conscience and confidence in God's loving mercy. It is also possible to imagine that a person could be physically relaxed while being spiritually agitated and desolate for one reason or another.

During a visit to Medjugorje I was impressed by two of the prophetic messages that were uttered on the Lord's behalf by the visionaries. I want to quote two of them. The first is for our everyday lives: 'If you want to be very happy, live a simple, humble life, pray a lot, and don't worry and fret over your problems, let them be settled by God.' The second message concerns the future: 'Don't think about wars, chastisements, evil. It is when you concentrate on these things that you are on the way to enter into them. Your responsibility is to accept divine peace, live it.'

TRUSTING IN DIVINE PROVIDENCE

The great German scripture scholar Joachim Jeremias has pointed to the fact that trusting faith was of central importance in Christ's teaching: 'In content Jesus' whole message is ... a call to faith, even if the word does not occur very often.' In the synoptic gospels, Jesus does not talk about faith in God's existence. Rather he talks, in typically Jewish fashion, about the exercise of trust in the concrete circumstances of everyday life. In a world that he knew to be dangerous and uncertain, Jesus highlighted a number of important points.

He declared: 'Blessed are the poor' (Lk 6:20) and 'How blessed are the poor in spirit' (Mt 5:3). In other words, blessed are those who, in their vulnerability and weakness, depend on God in all situations of need. People experience the pinch of radical need in a number of characteristic ways. To begin with, there is what is known as creature feeling. It is based on the awareness that nothing that exists, including, myself, is the adequate explanation of its own existence (cf. 2 Matt 7:8). Admittedly, most people are not consciously aware of this kind of fundamental anxiety but it is indirectly experienced in the following ways.

Firstly, there is the problem of material poverty. Poor people, especially in the third world, live on the margins of existence. In their relative powerlessness they have to depend on such things as the vagaries of the weather, governmental agencies and the generosity of others.

Secondly, in the developed world especially, there is what Mother Teresa referred to as the famine of the heart. It is often experienced in the form of problems such as feeling unwanted, loneliness and depression, together with neuroses, addictions and obsessions of different kinds.

Jesus believed that God has a *benevolent plan* for each of our lives. He agreed with Jeremiah who said: 'For surely I know the plans I have for you, says the Lord, plans for your welfare and not for harm, to give you a future and a hope' (Jer 29:11). That plan is expressed in three interrelated ways.

1. To begin with, there is our vocation in life whether married or single. For example, I discovered mine when, as a result of a religious experience, I decided to become a priest in 1963.

2. There is often a vocation within a vocation. For example, when I became a priest, I discovered an inner calling to preach, teach and write. Many people have a similar experience. After a time of searching they discover what they really want to do.

3. Then within the context of our vocation we are guided by the Spirit on a day to day basis. As Cardinal Newman wrote: 'Lead kindly light amid the encircling gloom. ... I do not ask to see the distant scene, one step enough for me.' Jesus taught that besides having a plan for our lives, *God provides* for us in our needs. God's provision is experienced in two main ways.

God's internal provision
The Lord provides for us *internally* in the form of natural talents and supernatural graces. If God calls a person to carry out some task, e.g. to be a preacher or teacher, the Lord gives them such things as a good education, retentive memory and good communication skills. God will also supply the graces needed to carry out the task. For example, more often than not, an effective preacher or teacher is granted the gifts of wisdom and knowledge (cf. Is 11:1; 1 Cor 12:8). As Paul says

in Phil 2:13, 'It is God who is at work in you, enabling you both to will and to work for his good pleasure.' In other words, not only does the Spirit guide us in accordance with God's will, the same Spirit enables us to carry it out, even when from a human point of view, it seems beyond our capability. I want to share a personal experience that taught me this lesson in no uncertain way.

Many years ago a number of us were conducting a parish mission in Dublin. It was around the time I experienced the burnout mentioned at the beginning of this book. I wasn't feeling well at the time. On one of the days – it happened to be my 40th birthday – I was relieved to find that I was neither appointed preacher or celebrant for that night. However, a few moments before the Eucharist was due to start, I was asked to say the mass. I can recall having a profound feeling of powerlessness and emptiness. Standing at the vesting bench I said a quiet prayer. 'Lord I am at the end of my tether. I am completely drained. I have nothing to offer. How can I lead your people in celebration? Unless you help me, my efforts will be in vain.'

After that, we went out to the sanctuary and mass began. When a colleague had preached the sermon, I approached the altar intending to begin the offertory prayers. Once again a feeling of powerlessness came over me. I silently repeated the words I had prayed in the sacristy, and proceeded with the blessing of the gifts. As I began to recite the Eucharistic prayers something happened. I became palpably aware of a mysterious presence. I was so moved by this consoling experience that, for a brief time, I couldn't speak. During this embarrassing pause I was amazed to find that there was an uncanny silence in the Church. There wasn't a sound. No one was coughing, shuffling or rustling paper. Evidently everyone was aware of the Presence. When I regained my composure, I said, 'I'm sure that you can all sense it. The Holy Spirit has come upon all of us, the Risen Lord is here!' As I continued the mass the sense of presence deepened. It was one of the most wonderful spiritual experiences of my life.

When the Eucharist ended, there were unusually long queues outside the confessionals. When people came in they said such things as, 'What on earth happened out there tonight? That was the happiest half hour I have ever experienced in my life... I wish it could have gone on and on... I feel that God has taken away many of my fears and given me his peace instead.'

What a paradox! When I was at my lowest ebb from a human point of view, I was granted one of the greatest blessings of my priestly life. Besides being the best birthday present I had ever received it taught me a number of things. If we are seeking to follow God's will, and to minister in his name, there is no need to be afraid. If we trust in his loving goodness we discover that Divine 'grace is sufficient for us, for God's power is made perfect in weakness... I can do everything through Him who gives me strength' (2 Cor 12:9; Phil 4:13). Nowadays when I face similar crucifixion points of powerlessness in my life, instead of anxiously wrestling with my fears, I try to nestle in the Lord through faith.

God's external provision

God's provision is experienced in external ways in the form of material benefits. As St Vincent de Paul said, 'We ought to have confidence in God that he will look after us since we know for certain that as long as we are grounded in that sort of love and trust we will always be under the protection of God in heaven, we will remain unaffected by evil and never lack what is needed when everything seems headed for disaster.' It is important to realise that there is nothing magical about God's provision. Normally the Lord acts in ordinary ways through secondary causes. In other words, God uses such things as other people, natural circumstances, coincidences and synchronicity in order to bless us. I want to illustrate how trust in God's provision can lead to blessing by sharing the following experience.

In 1997 I flew to Canberra in Australia to speak at a conference over the Pentecost weekend. On the way out I noticed that I was getting a sore throat. That worried me. I feared that it might cause me to have many fits of coughing. Soon after my arrival I got a bad dose of laryngitis. My voice got weak and husky. By the time the conference began, speaking was an increasing strain. By the Saturday afternoon my voice had disappeared completely. When I opened my mouth, not a single sound emerged. For the first time in my life I was utterly speechless and had to communicate in a whisper.

I decided to reflect and pray. I was mortified by the fact that I had come all this way, at great expense to my Australian hosts, and was unable to give all the scheduled talks. I poured out my feelings to the Lord and went through the four steps of the prayer exercise suggested by Agnes Sanford. At some point I recalled two verses from the bible which mean a lot to me. The first is from Prov 3:5, 'Trust in the Lord with all your heart and lean not on your own understanding,' and the second from Ps 37:5 , which says, 'Commit your way to the Lord; trust in him and he will act.' Then I said, 'Heavenly Father, I have travelled thousands of miles in order to preach your word. Now that I have no voice I am anxious and embarrassed. But I believe in your plan and provision for my life. I refuse to get frightened. I entrust this whole situation to you. I ask you to restore my voice, at least enough to be able to communicate with the help of the sound system. I cast all my anxieties upon you in the confident belief that you care about me, and I thank you that you hear my prayer in accordance with your promises.' I had a real sense of the presence, goodness and trustworthiness of the Lord, and felt that God would help me in my hour of need.

I got up in the morning, took a shower and tried to speak, but not a sound could I make. When it was obvious at breakfast that I was as dumb as Zechariah, a priest companion said he would give a substitute talk. After the meal was over I went to my room. I had a subjective conviction that despite all indications to the contrary, God would answer my prayers. So I went to the priest who had offered to speak in my stead and said in a whisper, 'When its time for the talk, I'd like to step forward to the microphone and try to speak. If I can't, you take over.' He agreed. When we got to the conference venue there was prayer and praise for about forty minutes. Then I stepped forward to the microphone. I felt like St Peter stepping out of the boat to walk on water. My chosen subject happened to be, 'Trusting in divine providence'. I opened my lips, trusted in God, and wonder of wonders I could speak. True my voice was weak and husky, but I could speak and the amplification compensated for my lack of volume. It was a very emotional moment for me. God my loving and ever faithful Father had heard my prayer, he had literally given me the gift of tongues. In the event I gave a fifty minute talk, preached a homily at the Eucharist and later on conducted a healing service. Since then the organisers have written to say that in spite of all my vicissitudes they had heard that many people were richly blessed during the conference.

All things work for good
Jesus believed that God's providence embraces evil and transforms it, much as the oyster transforms the irritating presence of grit within itself, into a beautiful pearl. No matter what weaknesses people have, what mistakes they make, or what sins they commit, they are integrated into God's plan and embraced by Divine providence. As a result they can become the birthplace of blessing. Evil doesn't have the last word, that word belongs to God, and it is a word of blessing and victory. God has plans A B C and D. Each one is as good if not better than the last. That is evident in the story of Joseph and his brothers. They are merciless when they betray their brother. Years later they have to travel to Egypt in order to seek food during a time of famine. Unbeknown to them Joseph is the man they have to deal with. Having revealed his identity to the brothers he says: 'Come close to me.' When they had done so, he said, 'I am your brother Joseph, the one you sold into Egypt! And now, do not be distressed and do not be angry with yourselves for selling me here, because it was to save lives that God sent me ahead of you.' (Gen 45:4-5). In other words God used the treachery of the brothers as a springboard for their own future blessing! Later on we would betray our brother Jesus, not into slavery but into death. But just as the misfortunes of Joseph led to blessing, so the death of Jesus leads to our salvation. St Paul grasped the nature of this paradoxical dynamic when he said: 'Where sin abounds the grace of God more abounds' (Rm 5:20). I'm convinced that those who develop a strong trust in divine providence are much less prone to anxiety than would otherwise be the case.

They are able to carry out the repeated command of scripture, 'do not be afraid.'

Seek first God's Kingdom

That is why Jesus said in Matt 6:25-34: 'Therefore I tell you, do not worry about your life, what you will eat or drink; or about your body, what you will wear. Is not life more important than food, and the body more important than clothes? Look at the birds of the air; they do not sow or reap or store away in barns, and yet your heavenly Father feeds them. Are you not much more valuable than they? Who of you by worrying can add a single hour to his life? And why do you worry about clothes? See how the lilies of the field grow. They do not labor or spin. Yet I tell you that not even Solomon in all his splendor was dressed like one of these. If that is how God clothes the grass of the field, which is here today and tomorrow is thrown into the fire, will he not much more clothe you, O you of little faith? So do not worry, saying, "What shall we eat?" or "What shall we drink?" or "What shall we wear?" For the pagans run after all these things, and your heavenly Father knows that you need them. But seek first his kingdom and his righteousness, and all these things will be given to you as well. Therefore do not worry about tomorrow, for tomorrow will worry about itself. Each day has enough trouble of its own.' The extent to which the self-centred ego dies in order to devote itself single-mindedly to God and the purposes of God, is the extent to which anxious fear will be replaced by inner peace. As Aldous Huxley observed in his *Perennial Philosophy,* 'Fear, worry, anxiety – these form the central core of industrialised selfhood. Fear cannot be got rid of by personal effort, but only by the ego's absorption in a cause greater than its own interests. Absorption in any cause will rid the mind of some of its fears; but only absorption in the loving and knowing of the divine Ground (i.e. God) can rid it of all fear.'

Scripture Texts for Times of Stress

The following scripture texts may provide you with guidance and strength in times of stress:

Joshua 1:9
'Remember that I have commanded you to be determined and confident! Don't be afraid or discouraged, for I, the Lord your God, am with you wherever you go'

Isaiah 41:10
'Fear not, for I am with you, be not dismayed, for I am your God; I will uphold you with my victorious right hand.'

2 Chronicles 20:15
'The Lord says that you must not be discouraged or be afraid the battle depends on God, not on you.'

Exodus 14:13–14
'Do not be afraid! Stand by and see the salvation of the Lord which he will accomplish for you today ... The Lord will fight for you while you keep silent.'

Jeremiah 17:7-9
'But I will bless the person who puts his trust in me. He is like a tree growing near a stream and sending out roots to the water. It is not afraid when hot weather comes, because its leaves stay green; it has no worries when there is no rain; it keeps on bearing fruit.'

2 Chronicles 14:11
'Yahweh, no one but you can stand up for the powerless against the powerful. Come to our help. Yahweh our God! We rely on you, and confront this crisis in your name. Yahweh, you are our God. Let man leave everything to you.'

Daniel 10:17-20
'For now I have no strength, and no breath is left in me. Again one having the appearance of a man touched me and strengthened me. And he said: 'Oh, man greatly beloved, fear not, peace be with you; be strong and of good courage.'

John 16:13
'You will have peace by being united to me. The world will make you suffer. But be brave! I have overcome the world.'

Romans 8:31
'If God is for us, who is against us?'

Hebrews 13:5-7
'The Lord has said: I will never fail you nor forsake you. Hence we confidently say: "The Lord is my helper, I will not be afraid; what can man do to me?"'

1 Peter 5:7
'Cast all your anxieties on the Lord because he cares about you

Psalm 34:18
'The Lord is near the brokenhearted, and saves the crushed in spirit.'

Matthew 11:29-30
'Come to me, all who labour and are heavily laden, and I will give you rest. Take my yoke upon you, and learn from me, for I am gentle and humble of heart, and you will find rest for your souls.'

Prayer of St Teresa of Avila

Let nothing perturb you,
Nothing frighten you,
All things pass.
God does not change.
Patience achieves everything.
Whoever has God, lacks nothing.
God alone suffices.

Reflection Questions

1. What causes you stress?

   _____

   _____

2. Are you too concerned with what other people think, and do you
   have an overweening desire to please?
   Yes _____   No _____

3. Do you think that you are lovable for what you do, not for who
   you are?
   Yes _____   No _____

4. How do you deal with hurt and anger?

   _____

   _____

5. Do you tend to adopt a 'peace-at-any-price' approach by burying
   it alive?
   Yes _____   No _____

6. Do you become aggressive with others?
   Yes _____   No _____

7. Are you assertive?
   Yes _____   No _____

8. Do you establish priorities for yourself and stick to them?

Yes _____ No _____

9. Do you live in the present, one day at a time?

Yes _____ No _____

10. You care for many people and give out energy to them. What are the sources of your energy?

_____

_____

11. You care for many people. Who really cares for you?

_____

_____

12. What form of relaxation exercise do you think you could use in the future?

_____

_____

_____

13. What form of physical exercise could you realistically hope to engage in on a regular basis in the future?

_____

_____

_____

14. What form of recreation could you reasonably expect to engage in on a regular basis in the future?

_____

_____

_____

15. If you were to list three long time priorities for yourself over the next year, what would they be? List them in order of importance.

_____

_____

_____

16. If you were to list three short time priorities for the period before Christmas, what would they be? List them in order of importance.

_____

_____

_____

Resources

Al-Anon Family Groups
Room 5, Capel Street,Dublin
Tel 01-8732699
www.al-anon.alateen.orh/alalist_world.html

Alcoholics Anonymous
109 South Circular Road, Dublin 8
Tel 01-4538998/Fax 01- 4538998
www.alcoholicsanonymous.ie/index.html

Accord (marriage counselling)
Tel 01-4784400
admin@accord.ie
www.accord.ie

Aware (emotional problems)
147 Phibsboro Road, Dublin 7
Tel 01-6766166/Fax 01-8306840
www.iol.ie/aware

Separated Persons Association of Ireland
Carmichael House, North Brunswick Street, Dublin 7
Tel 01-8720684

Gamblers Anonymous
Carmichael House, North Brunswick Street, Dublin 7
Tel 01-8721133

Amen (domestic violence – men)
9-10 Academy Street, Navan, Co Meath
Tel 046-23718/Fax 046-23718
www.amen.ie

Gingerbread (one-parent families)
Carmichael House, North Brunswick Street, Dublin 7
Tel 01-6710291/Fax 01-8146619
www.gingerbread.ie

Faoiseamh (victims of abuse by clergy or religious)
Freephone 1800-331234

Family Mediation Service
1st Floor, St Stephen's Green House, Earlsfort Terrace, Dublin 2
Tel 01-6344320/Fax 01-6622339
www.oasis.gov.ie/relationships/family_mediation_service/general.html

Parentline
Carmichael House, North Brunswick Street, Dublin 7
Tel 01-8733500/Helpline 1890-927277
www.parentline.net

Samaritans
Tel (ROI)1850-609 090/Tel (NI) 08457-989090
www.samaritans.org

The National Suicide Bereavement Support Network
www.nsbns.org

Aoibhneas (domestic violence – women)
Tel 01-8670701
www.aoibhneas.org

Victim Support
Haliday House, 32 Arran Quay, Dublin 7
Tel 01-6798673 / Fax 01-8780944
www.victimsupport.ie / join.html

Mental Health Ireland
Mensana House, 6 Adelaide Street, Dún Laoghaire, Co. Dublin
Tel 01-2841166 / Fax 01-2841736
www.mentalhealthireland.ie

USEFUL INTERNET SITES

- There are many sites on the internet that provide useful information on the subject of stress. There is a simple, brief but useful one at www.mindtools.com / smpage.html

- There is another, more comprehensive site that contains many articles on different aspects of stress at www.selfgrowth.com / stress.html

- The Voluntary Health Insurance of Ireland have a helpful site at www.vhihealthe.com which has useful information and a stress test.

- The Health and Safety Authority has a useful site entitled 'Workplace Stress, Causes, Effects, Control,' at www.has.ie / osh / stress.htm

Psychology Self-Help Resources on the Internet (a large helpful site, with a section entitled 'Anxiety, Fears, Stress, Panic, Trauma, Dissociation') can be found at www.psywww.com / resource / selfhelp.htm

USEFUL BOOKS

Joe Armstrong, *Workplace Stress in Ireland* (Dublin: Irish Congress of
Trade Unions, 2001)

Herbert Benson, *Beyond the Relaxation Response* (London: Fount
Paperbacks, 1985)

G. Nathan, E. Straats, P. Rosch, *The Doctor's Guide to Instant Stress
Relief* (New York: Ballentine, 1991)

Martha Davis et al., *The Relaxation & Stress Reduction Workbook*
(Oakland CA: New Harbinger, 2000)

Brian Lomas, *Stress and Time Management* (Chichester: Summersdale
Publishers, 2001)

Cary L. Cooper, Stephen Palmer *Conquer Your Stress* (London:
Chartered Institute of Personnel and Development, 2000)

British Medical Association, Family Doctor Series, ed. by Tony
Smith, *Stress* (Dorling Kindersley, 1999)

Jeff Davidson, *The Complete Idiot's Guide to Managing Stress*
(Indianapolis: Alpha Books, 1999).

Edmund Bourne, *The Anxiety & Phobia Workbook* (Oakland CA: New
Harbinger, 2000)

For a full and comprehensive booklist see the International Stress
Management Association's website, www.isma.org.uk/booklist.htm